DATE DUE FOR RETURN

Allerton Library

LEN GOODMAN

MY LOST LONDON

A personal journey

LEN GOODMAN

MY LG1
LOST
LONDON

A personal journey

Trinity Mirror Media

I'd like to dedicate this book to Grandad Albert, my Grandma, and my Mum; as well as all the other East End people who love London just as much as I do. But always remember – we got what we wanted, but miss what we had.

Trinity Mirror Media

MY LOST LONDON
By Len Goodman

Editor: Richard Havers
Design: Graeme Halliwell, Colin Harrison, Ben Renshaw
Production: Adam Oldfield, Harri Aston

Photography: Mirrorpix, Martin Spaven, Len Goodman's personal collection
Copyright text: Trinity Mirror Media / Len Goodman

Published by Trinity Mirror Media

Managing Director: Ken Rogers. Senior Editor: Steve Hanrahan
Editor: Paul Dove. Senior Art Editor: Rick Cooke
Senior Marketing Executive: Claire Brown
Senior Book Sales Executive: Karen Cadman

First Edition
Published in Great Britain in 2013.
Published and produced by: Trinity Mirror Media,
PO Box 48, Old Hall Street, Liverpool L69 3EB.

ISBN: 9781908695581

Printed and bound by CPI Colour, Croydon, CR0 4YY

Join me on a special journey

I was almost born within the sound of Bow Bells, nearly born in Wales, but ended up being born in Kent. But never mind all that, I'm a Londoner, through and through.

I spent my early childhood in Bethnal Green and even when we moved to live across the other side of the Thames, I spent as much time as I could in the East End. I worked on the docks in London, played football all over London and once I took up dancing, I was forever travelling around London.

Like every person my age, I'm nostalgic for what's no longer around. Don't get me wrong, I don't think it was all much better in the ol' days but it does get on my wick when some of the best things about life before the internet are in danger of being forgotten.

What do I miss? Well, I think lots of kids miss doing all the things we could do when I was growing up. I miss the characters, the markets, how we made our own fun and, once I was old enough, the old boozers or a trip up the wild West End for a real night out.

I love walking around London, seeing what's changed. I remember where buildings or even whole streets used to be, the old markets, like Covent Garden and Spitalfields, where I used to go dancing above Burton's The Tailors or down the Palais.

This book gives me the chance to take you back to the London I remember as a kid, as a teenager and as a young man about town. Remembering all that was great about London will help bring back some of the good times that we had back in the last century.

CONTENTS

1. My London Childhood   10

2. A Sporting Life   44

3. Down The Market   66

4. Dock Life   98

5. That's Entertainment   110

6. Dancing Feet   128

7. The Way We Lived Then   146

8. London's Transport   184

9. Building Sights   206

10. Up West   224

No Place Like Home   239

CHAPTER

1

MY LONDON CHILDHOOD

I have always felt lucky to have grown up in London when I did. I was born in 1944 and missed most of the hardships brought on by World War Two. With the post-war changes that occurred, I got to experience so much and had the benefit of spending time with my mum and dad in Kent and up the East End with my grandad and nan – it was like two childhoods rolled into one . . .

Adolf spoiled my London birthday

I BLAME Adolf Hitler. If it weren't for him I would have been born in Whitechapel, within the sound of Bow Bells. As it is, I was born in Farnborough in Kent, which is also the county in which I've lived most of my life. Despite this, I still consider myself a Londoner and, of course, when I open my mouth, everyone thinks I am!

Truth is, I was very nearly born in Wales! In early 1944, Dad and Mum were living in a little village called Felinfoel, about 10 miles from RAF Pembrey, which is near Llanelli in South Wales, where my father was working as an electrician, mostly at airfields, maintaining the lights and other electrical equipment.

A doctor sent my mum to Swansea to have me but there were no beds, so she got on the train and headed for home. When she finally arrived at The London Hospital in Whitechapel, they decided that it was safer to send her to Kent, because there had been a massive air raid the night before. All of which explains how I ended up being born in Farnborough on April 25, 1944.

I spent my first seven years living in a two-up, two-down in Harold Street, Bethnal Green. Although ours was the end of the row and had three bedrooms – very des res. My mum and dad lived there with my mum's family and it really was an amazing household. My grandad was a costermonger, a barrow boy who started out with a stall in Bethnal Green market before eventually owning two London shops, along with another my mum ran in Kent.

However, when I came along there was just the barrow. I went to Cranbrook School in 1949, a couple of streets away from Harold Street, in a four-storey building with the playground on the roof – it was all netted and fenced to stop us falling off.

During my first few days at school I remember a boy being sent home because he didn't have any shoes to wear. The school's no longer there now but the building still is and has been converted into a block of flats. Harold Street is gone too and in its place are several blocks of flats.

One thing I have to thank my grandad for is that he was the one that gave me so many funny sayings, some of which I've even used when critiquing dancers on the television.

"It's freezing cold out, you'd better wear two hairnets," is what he'd say to my nan. Another time he said, "Lou," – my nan's name was Louisa, like my mum – "This toast is as hard as a beggar boy's arse."

I suppose it's because a beggar boy sat on the hard cold ground, but whether it was something he made up or just heard from someone, I've no idea. It's a shame I never thought to ask him at the time, but how many of us have regrets like that?

What's important is that I have very fond memories of growing up in a very different London from the London of today.

"THIS WAS MY FIRST CAR.
I'M POSING WITH BUBBA MILLER
AND HIS SISTER IN FRONT OF OUR
OUTSIDE TOILET IN HAROLD STREET"

"MANY CHILDREN WERE EVACUATED. I STAYED PUT, I WAS TOO YOUNG TO LEAVE MY MUM"

I turned up in the 'Baby Blitz'

THE Blitz began in September 1940 and lasted until May 1941 with around two million homes destroyed in Britain, 1.2 million of which were in London. Almost 40,000 were killed and more than 50,000 people were seriously injured.

The majority of those who lost their lives were in London. The devastation to the City of London was terrible with 30% of this historic area totally destroyed. The East End of London, including Bethnal Green, was severely damaged.

During the bombing of London, as many as 136,000 people slept each night in underground stations, although the number reduced from its peak in October 1940 to around 96,000 in January 1941. The numbers of people made

homeless in the Blitz was enormous, and for some unfortunate people it happened more than once. I was born during what became known as the 'Baby Blitz', an offensive launched in January 1944 that ran until the night before I was born.

Nearly two months after I came along, and a week after the D-Day landings in June 1944, the watchers at Royal Observer Corps station in Kent's Romney Marshes saw a strange glowing black object in the sky heading towards them – they had never seen anything like it before. Within weeks it was to become all too familiar – it was the first V-1 rocket. Of the 10 that were fired that first day, four made it across the channel and only one managed to make

One of the two V-2 rockets that landed on Bethnal Green on February 8, 1945. We were lucky, just down the road East Ham had 14 V-2s, Ilford had 35 and Barking 21. There were also nine Doodlebugs that hit Bethnal Green

A V-1 hit in Underwood Street, Shoreditch, just down the road from Bethnal Green in August 1944

A German V-1 flying bomb on exhibition in Piccadilly in October 1944

it to London, where it crash-landed on Grove Road in Hackney, killing six people. It was the start of a different, but in some ways even more frightening, Blitz. By the end of June, 'Doodlebugs' or 'buzz-bombs' as they were known, were hitting London at a rate of around 80 every day.

In all, more than 9,000 Doodlebugs were fired against Britain but less than 40% managed to reach their target, nevertheless more than 6,000 people were killed in London and a further 18,000 were injured.

In September 1944, the increasingly desperate Nazi regime pressed into service the unstoppable V-2 Rocket. Weighing almost 13,000 kilograms, they came down from the stratosphere at 3,000 miles per hour – with no warning. These were psychologically more potent than the V-1s but less effective against the civilian population, but only due to the fact that many fewer were fired against London and they had navigational and reliability problems. In all, around 2,700 people were killed and 6,000 injured by the 520 V-2s that hit London, with attacks continuing until 27 March, 1945, when 34-year-old Mrs Ivy Millichamp became the last British civilian to die in an air raid at her home in Orpington in Kent.

Such was the threat that the Government even considered evacuating London. Fortunately, the advancing Allies captured the majority of the V-1 and V-2 launch sites.

This could have been us; only this was taken in 1945

There were bomb sites all over London and lots around Bethnel Green. Halfway along Harold Street a bomb had dropped, this was an area we used to call the glory bumps; we were told not to ride our bikes over it in case there were any unexploded bombs.

Opposite, there was an area of open ground that was mostly grassed over but there was also a large area of tarmac.

At one end of the tarmac were two low brick walls that stood slightly above the tarmac and were about nine feet apart. This used to be the entrance to an air raid shelter.

One day in about 1953, probably just after the Coronation, my mates and me thought we'd try digging out the entrance to the shelter.

We spent several days removing quite a lot of soil until we finally got to expose the whole of a wooden door about eight or 10 steps below the surface. We were about to try getting behind the door, despite someone raising the idea that there might be dead Germans in there, when a copper came along Harold Street: "What are you boys up to?" "Nuffink," said the oldest boy.

"Well if it's nothing you better clear off hadn't you? Go on, be off home," said the policeman.

We never did get inside to see what was there...

Bomb sites were adapted for all kinds of games, as can be seen at this one just off Bow Road in the East End

"WE WERE TOLD NOT TO RIDE OUR BIKES OVER THE 'GLORY BUMPS' IN CASE THERE WERE ANY UNEXPLODED BOMBS"

You can't beat an outdoor bath

THESE kids bathing in a horse trough in 1957 made me think two things.

I bet lots of people under a certain age have no idea what these things are when they come across one of the few that are left dotted around London.

It also reminds me of my early introduction to bathing. In our back yard at Harold Street we had a boiler that was used for cooking the beetroot we sold on the stall. Nan was in charge of the boiler and cooling beetroot. Underneath the copper boiler was a large metal ring with eight burners that was connected by a long

pipe to the gas supply, somewhere in the house. Besides cooking the beetroot in it, Nan also used it for doing the family's washing. As the water was heating up, before she put the beetroot in, Nan would strip me off and put me in the water while it was still tepid. She'd give me a bloody good scrubbing down while I stood in the cauldron – I must have looked a bit like a cannibal's lunch.

After I got out, the water was heated some more and then in would go the beetroot for cooking. Customers always commented on how good Grandad's beetroot tasted.

These children are trying to cool off in the summer of 1949 in the East End somewhere – still not as much fun as the beetroot boiler!

"NAN WOULD GIVE ME A BLOODY GOOD SCRUBBING DOWN WHILE I STOOD IN THE CAULDRON…AFTER I GOT OUT, THE WATER WAS HEATED SOME MORE AND THEN IN WOULD GO THE BEETROOT FOR COOKING"

Sweets were treats

After sweet rationing ended in 1949 there were still shortages on some things going into the 1950s. These kids were looking excited at the prospect of spending their money. The thing was, we didn't have that much money to buy sweets so we were rationed by cash as much as by supply.

These kids, seen here in 1947, are using an old bomb site, cleared of its rubble as an area to grow vegetables. It is a bit like the Dig For Victory idea; in some ways having been victorious didn't always feel like it, things were still in short supply

Away from the sweet shops we had some very unsophisticated vending machines. There was always one on a station platform, or so it seemed

This Soapbox Grand Prix was held in Brighton in 1950

Woolwich boys prepare for Soapbox Derby in August 1954

Racing on old pram wheels

DID you know there are still soapbox derbies held in Britain?

Today, it's a relatively sophisticated sport with modern soapboxes that are all shiny and hi-tech. We used to make soapboxes out of old pram wheels and just stick a box on the top.

In the late 1940s and early 1950s it became very popular, especially with the Scouts who were behind some big races like the annual event they held in Brighton.

What I really liked doing was skateboard racing. These too were nothing like the things you see today, ours were just a flat piece of board we rested on a roller skate and then found a convenient hill to race down. I was forever coming off and taking the skin off my knees.

Boys love making things. We would build our own racing karts. It could be the pit at Silverstone but it's an inner-street production line in June 1950

This race was held in Fore Street, in the City of London. Apparently, this was the Blitz area finals ahead of the grand final in Scarborough, Yorkshire in 1946

"THIS WAS BEFORE MY TIME AS IT WAS
THE WHITSUN HOLIDAY IN MAY 1926, BUT
IT WAS JUST THE SORT OF THING THAT
HAPPENED, EVEN POST-WAR. THERE WAS
A LOT MORE FREEDOM"

As kids we had our whole year sorted

WHEN I was growing up there was an unwritten set of rules by which we lived our lives, rules that mapped out the whole year for us and, best of all, they gave us variety.

In September and October it was the conker season. Then, for some inexplicable reason, came fag cards – the cards that came free in cigarette packets and later with tea. We would spend hours flicking cards against a wall trying to win our mate's cards and him trying to win yours.

We did, of course, also play cricket and football in the street at Bethnal Green or down the recreation ground near Blackfen. In between we also had miniature cricket that was played using a marble and miniature bat and regular marbles.

These girls are playing mums with their dolls and toy prams on the corner of Peace Street, formerly Artillery Street, in Bethnal Green in July 1939. It was just the same after the war, kids played on the streets on any day that it wasn't raining

I never did it but lots of my mates went train spotting; these kids are at Waterloo Station in August 1952. You occasionally see old blokes at stations writing down the numbers of trains but never kids anymore. Just another thing that's changed I guess

"CRICKET WAS BRIEFLY INTERRUPTED BY WIMBLEDON, IF YOU WERE LUCKY ENOUGH TO HAVE TENNIS RACKETS"

Kids swimming in the Thames in June 1952. It's never something I did but I'm sure it's something you never see today

Street cricket in 1950

Conkers at school in 1950. Do kids really have to wear protective goggles to play this today, or is it an urban myth?

Hi-Ho Silver . . . Away!

WHEN I saw this set of photographs it brought back so many memories; most of all it reminded me how we used to have to make our own fun.

The kid dressed in the cowboy hat, I think he is supposed to be a Canadian Mountie, was just one other reminder of how we used to all love watching cowboy films or TV series like Hopalong Cassidy or The Lone Ranger and Tonto. The TV we watched was more innocent and less violent, that's for sure.

"WE USED TO ALL LOVE WATCHING COWBOY FILMS OR TV SERIES LIKE HOPALONG CASSIDY OR THE LONE RANGER AND TONTO"

This series of photos was taken near Bow Road in the East End in 1954; I wonder where they all are now and what they are doing?

Buns and bins: My Coronation currant crisis

IN the summer of 1953, I was staying with my nan at Harold Street when she said there was going to be a street party to celebrate the Coronation of the Queen.

Just about every street in Bethnal Green had a party and each street wanted to outdo every other street. Harold Street was about a 100 yards long and in every house there were kids.

There were trestle tables laid out the length of the road, there was bunting hanging from house to house; every seat was filled with an expectant kid. The first course was a currant bun, which was and still is one of my favourites; not so much back then, the buns, it was the currants that I loved. I carefully ate the bun and made a small pile of currants on one side of my plate; I was saving the best until last. I watched as my pile of currants grew but I also noticed that some kids had wolfed theirs down in a matter of seconds. It was the mums' jobs to clear the tables after each course and, just as I was about to finish my bun and start on my currants, one of the mums came along. "What? You don't like currants luv'." In the blink of an eye my precious pile of currants was brushed into a bin.

I was devastated but luckily at that moment the sausages and beans arrived. As they did, all the kids started shouting out "Yum, Yum, pig's bum." We always said that for some reason before tucking in. What was truly amazing to us kids was that we could have as many sausages as we liked, not just one or two. There were huge frying pans over open fires full of great big fat sausages. For kids, still used to living in a world of rationing, this was nothing short of miraculous.

While we were still eating, a man did conjuring tricks. This was followed by jelly and blancmange. It was all washed down with gallons, or so it seemed, of lemonade and cream soda.

My grandad provided fruit, which was laid out all along the table. There were apples, oranges, pears and bananas. Some kids had never even seen a banana, let alone eaten one. I had to explain to one boy that you didn't eat the skin.

But all in all my overriding memory of the Queen's Coronation is – eat your currants quickly. I'm convinced that's why I eat so fast today – I'm worried about someone nicking my currants!

This wasn't our street party but it could easily have been. I'm glad to see that street parties still happen. It's a great way of bringing people together, especially as people living close to one another in London are not so familiar with their neighbours as we all were

A lemonade with Grandad outside the pub

FROM when we first moved to Kent I'd still spend a lot of my school holidays back in Bethnal Green, often staying all week at Nan and Grandad's. To get there I would take the train from Welling to London Bridge and then get on a number 8A bus.

"Now Lenny, tell the conductor you want to get off at the Salmon and Ball," said Mum. The pub, which is still there and looks much the same, is on Bethnal Green Road very close to where Grandad had his original shop.

This wasn't Grandad's local though, his was The Beehive, which was on the corner of Harold Street and the Old Roman Road, it was a proper workingmen's pub – a spit and sawdust, and Grandad never went anywhere else – nor did other people, you stuck to your 'local'. There would always be someone playing the old Joanna (piano) while men hung around the dartboard waiting for a game. Almost everyone smoked, mostly roll-ups, so there was always a fug in the pub. Sometimes he would take me down there and I would have to sit outside drinking lemonade, kids were not allowed in pubs.

A typical scene at a London pub (above) with the kids hanging around outside in July 1946. Right: A typical East End Pub in July 1963

"BEING BACK OUTSIDE THE SALMON AND BALL BRINGS IT ALL BACK. IT'S STILL VERY DEAR TO MY HEART ... CHEERS!"

These amazing horses used to deliver beer to Young's Brewery pubs. There was a time when all pubs had their beer delivered by a horse-drawn wagon

The Blind Beggar public house on Whitechapel was close to Bethnal Green and was one of the infamous haunts of the Kray Twins, the East End gang leaders who also lived in Bethnal Green. I never knew them and by the time this pub had gained notoriety in March 1966 when a rival gang member was shot and killed, for which crime Ronald Kray was convicted and was given life imprisonment, I had long moved away

The Dome of Discovery from across the Thames as well as the outline of the Royal Festival Hall under construction in 1950. Below: Men working on the dome. Not a hard hat in sight!

A new world at . . . SEVEN!

THE Festival of Britain was an amazing feat as I came to discover later.

Being taken there as a seven-year-old was very exciting, a bit like entering into a brave new world where anything seemed possible.

Today, because of what happened on the South Bank of the Thames, people have come to associate the festival with London, yet it took place throughout the country, from Inverness to Bournemouth. The centrepiece of the festival was on the South Bank and at Battersea Pleasure Gardens. The government's idea was to give Britain a sense of recovery after the war and offer a glimpse into the technology, science, design, architecture and the arts that people could look forward to.

The festival took place in 1951 but Winston Churchill's government demolished most of the site, on the South Bank, when it came to power in the autumn of that year, as they saw it as a Labour-inspired event.

Left: *The boating lake at Battersea Pleasure Gardens*

Right: *It could almost be me! Richard Huws designed this fountain*

"AN AERIAL VIEW OF THE FESTIVAL
OF BRITAIN EXHIBITION SITE.
IT WAS SO EXCITING GOING THERE.
IT FELT LIKE A WORLD WHERE
ANYTHING SEEMED POSSIBLE"

The 1966 World Cup final at the old Wembley Stadium in July 1966. Something that we will probably never see again and it was all down to three players from my beloved West Ham, Bobby Moore, Martin Peters and Geoff Hurst

2

Sport has always been a big part of my life and all over London there are places where sport was once played but is no longer. The way we play and watch sport is so different today than when I was growing up; for a start there are whole television channels dedicated to sport. In the 1950s and 1960s, you were lucky if you got to see the FA Cup final, the Derby and the Boat Race on the TV. If you wanted sport you had to 'be there' or, as many of us did, you played sport . . .

Football gave me my dancing break

Can you spot me? It's my old school football team and I'm on the back row, third from the right

AT senior school I played football and cricket. At Westwood Secondary Modern in Kent I played for the under-13s cricket team. In one game, always the grudge match, against Chislehurst and Sidcup Grammar School, I caught their leading batsman.

I say caught but in actual fact he hit the ball so hard that I didn't get my hand out of the way quick enough and the ball kind of lodged there and somehow I didn't drop it.

I was fielding next to my pal, Pete Dawson, and we were both so excited that we started whooping and hollering and jumping around. Having dismissed their danger man, we knew we were in with a good chance of winning and we did. The next day in assembly the headmaster stood on stage in front of the whole school and said, unexpectedly: "Goodman and Dawson please come here." We walked forward smiling, anticipating his congratulations for our fine performance the previous day.

"Goodman and Dawson, I understand from the sports master that there was disgusting behaviour on the cricket pitch. You both acted in a very unsporting like manner and because of this you will take no further part in any cricket for the rest of the season."

And that was it, we didn't, and all for showing some excitement at what we had done. It's one of those enduring memories of my school days that always remind me of how much times have changed.

It was football that got me into ballroom dancing, in a roundabout kind of way. When I left school and was an apprentice I was football crazy. I was in a five-a-side team, a Saturday side and a Sunday side. I also used to train three times a week so my life was going to work, playing football and a Saturday and Sunday out with a girl.

I was playing for Slade Green United on Hackney Marshes when I broke a metatarsal bone in my foot – the same one that every other footballer seems to break these days. I kicked the ball north while at the same time the biggest centre-half in the world tried to kick the ball south (well that's my story and I'm sticking to it).

"I KICKED THE BALL NORTH WHILE AT THE SAME TIME THE BIGGEST CENTRE HALF IN THE WORLD TRIED TO KICK THE BALL SOUTH"

The outcome was my foot went west and I was in agony for weeks. It was not only black and blue and nasty looking but was also the size of a Chinese wrestler's crotch. All the doctor said was: "Try to keep off of it as much as possible." This was ludicrous, as I still had to go to work, so I spent my life hobbling around. The foot was incredibly slow to heal and I went back to my doctor but ended up seeing a locum – an old Scottish doctor.

"You'll need to build your foot up a lot more before you can play again. Laddie, you could try dancing."

"Dancing?" I couldn't believe it.

"Aye lad, you need to keep that foot working, you need to exercise it and so dancing is my recommendation."

Later that day, the girl I was seeing drove me round my dad's place and he immediately said: "That's lucky, there's a new beginners' ballroom class starting next Tuesday."

Despite my thinking 'no way', the following Tuesday I was at Erith Dance Studio and a whole new world was about to be opened up to me.

It was not just cricket and football that were a big part of my younger life. Like many people that lived in the East End, boxing was too, and my uncles were professional fighters.

My grandad went dog racing regularly and like any self-respecting young lad from around Bethnal Green, I was a West Ham supporter … I still am!

Hackney Marshes, the scene
of my infamous accident,
taken from the air in 1980

Not pitch 67 again!

THIS photo taken on a Sunday in 1962 shows just how busy Hackney Marshes was. I'm sure I must be in the photograph somewhere! The trick was not to get changed too early for your game, as the first ones ready had to carry the posts and crossbar to the pitch.

Sometimes you were on pitch number 67, which was miles away! On any given Sunday during the season there were more than a hundred matches played on Hackney Marshes.

It was originally a marsh but was drained in medieval times and further changed when building rubble from bombing during World War Two was dumped at the site.

When the 2012 Olympic Park was built, it occupied some of the area on which there were football pitches.

These days there are just 82 football pitches during the winter, as well as cricket pitches during the summer.

On this January Sunday in 1962, there were 111 games, which meant 2,442 players along with 333 referees and linesmen – that's 11-a-side, because back then we didn't have substitutes

"THE TRICK WAS NOT TO GET CHANGED TOO EARLY FOR YOUR GAME, AS THE FIRST ONES READY HAD TO CARRY THE POSTS AND CROSSBAR TO THE PITCH"

A big family hit

BOXING was popular in our family, as it was all over London and especially East London. Mum had two cousins, Harry and Dickie Corbett, who had been boxing champions. Harry was the older but Dickie the more successful.

When Dickie won some money from the fight game, he opened a snooker hall in Bethnal Green Road, not far from where Grandad had his fruit and veg stall.

He put Harry in charge of the hall even though, or perhaps because, he was a little punch-drunk from having taken too many beatings while he had been fighting.

Dickie would sometimes come round to the Harold Street house where Dad and him would spar in the back yard. Now my father was my size, about 14 stone, six feet tall and he'd done a little bit of boxing, although never professionally. Dickie on the other hand was a bantamweight, who weighed about eight-and-a-half stone. He also had a lisp. According to my dad it was like being punched by a horse. His fists were lightning fast and when he caught you with a punch, you knew all about it.

My dad was mad on snooker and one day he was playing on a table when two spivs came in to the hall. They were big guys, dressed the part in camel coats and trilby hats. Once they started playing they also started taking the mick out of Harry Corbett. They asked for a cup of tea and because Harry walked a little funny they started telling him not to spill it. As time went along they became even more ugly. Later, as Harry was bringing over another cup of tea he spilled some of it on one of the two spivs. One of them got really nasty.

"I hear you used to be a fighter, bit effin' pathetic now ain't yer."

With that the other spiv stuck up his fists as if to square up to Harry.

"Come on you stupid worthless git, show us what yer made of."

In an instant, Harry went from being a shambling shadow of a boxer to the real thing; his fists came up whereupon he hit this guy with such force that he literally did a somersault over the snooker table landing in a heap on the floor on the other side. He was out cold; my dad said it was like something out of a film.

Below: The Blackfriars boxing arena, where Dickie and Harry Corbett fought regularly during the pre-war years. This photo was taken in April 1935

Bottom: Twenty-one-year old Joe Bugner on the left fighting the Canadian Bill Drover at Bethnal Green's York Hall in February 1971; it ended in a draw. Years later, when I was playing golf with Henry Cooper, he said to me: "Joe was knocked down so many times he had a cauliflower arse."

*Randolph Turpin beat
Sugar Ray Robinson, who
was undefeated in 91 fights
since 1943, in London to
win the world middleweight
title on 14 January 1951*

When I was a teenager I'd go with my mates to York Hall to watch the boxing.

We used to decide which boxer we would support; often it was a random as "let's shout for the guy in the blue shorts", after which we would cheer him on for the whole match. On one occasion when we did this, our guy won and afterwards the loser leant over the ropes and shouted at us.

"Hey, you shouted for the other bloke and I've got a boil on my neck!"

I'd been introduced to boxing when I was about seven. We were staying at my nan's caravan in Clacton and my dad woke me up to listen to Britain's Randolph Turpin's world title fight with American Sugar Ray Robinson on the wireless from America; it had been the talk of the sporting world for weeks before. Turpin had beaten Robinson in London in January but lost the rematch in New York in September 1951.

EVENT | ROUND |

Earls Court was the scene of numerous major boxing matches in London. Seen here is the preparation for the fight between American Joey Maxim and defending world champion Freddie Mills on 24 January 1950. Mills was making his first defence against underdog Maxim. The American won by knockout in the 10th round and after the fight three of Mills' teeth were found embedded in Maxim's left glove. Mills never fought again

Going to the dogs

THERE used to be greyhound racing tracks all over London and my grandad was a regular.

In 1966, during the World Cup, the owners of Wembley Stadium refused to cancel regular greyhound racing, which meant the match between Uruguay and France was played at White City. White City was a very popular dog track that finally closed in 1984. There were once 33 greyhound stadiums in the London area, now there are only three left, at Crayford, Romford and Wimbledon.

The White City greyhound track, September 1946

This scene in the tote office shows the way the betting slips were kept in the pre-computer days. It was a labour-intensive operation

Catford greyhound track in 1950. Opened in 1932, it closed in 2003

Olympic spirit lives on

WHITE City Stadium was for years one of the largest stadiums in the UK until the last event at the stadium, a greyhound race on the 22 September 1984.

It was originally built for the 1908 Olympic Games and was part of a 140-acre complex of palaces and exhibition buildings for the Franco-British exhibition. Most of the buildings had whitewashed exteriors, which is why it became known as White City.

The stadium originally held 93,000 people and during the Olympics it hosted the athletics, football, and cycling events, as well as the finish of the first modern marathon. For nearly 20 years it was hardly used until it was taken over by the Greyhound Racing Association in 1927 and from then on mainly hosted greyhound racing and speedway.

The ladies' archery competition at the White City stadium in 1908

The finish of the 120-yard dash during the 1908 Olympic Games at White City Stadium

One of the earliest Olympic dramas to be captured on camera was when Italian marathon runner Pietri Dorando, who crossed the finish line in first place, was disqualified after he was helped back on to his feet by race officials after collapsing during the final lap

A Mini Grand Prix at White City Stadium in March 1975

The mighty Hammers

I'VE been a West Ham supporter all my life, through thick and thin. Admittedly, there's been a bit more thin than thick but, as a football fan, you have to get used to that.

When I was a kid and went to Upton Park, the men would pass you to the front over their heads so you could get a better view.

When I got older and went to games, I stood in the area of the ground known as the 'Chicken Run', which was an old wooden stand (standing room only) on the east side of the pitch. It was surrounded by the kind of wire that you used on chicken runs.

Every year after I started work I would put a £1 bet on West Ham winning the cup. Usually the odds were about 20-1 in those days. I was earning £2 3 shillings a week when I started as an apprentice in 1959, although it did go up by 10 shillings when I reached 16. When we won the cup in 1964, I reckon I was probably earning around £6 a week, so the £20 I won was fantastic.

Upton Park, April 9, 1959. I'm sure I must be there somewhere!

Fans queue at Upton Park as tickets for their FA Cup match against Fulham in February 1958 go on sale. These days no-one ever stands in line for tickets, they just phone up or go online

A 17-year-old Bobby Moore pictured alongside teammates Andy Smillie (left) and Tony Scott (right) before the start of the 1958-59 season. Bobby was one of my all-time heroes. He made his first-team debut the following month against Manchester United on August 5, 1958

Upton Park closed on Boxing Day 1962 due to a cold spell. It's not something you see at Premiership games with under-floor heating and all the other modern facilities that are on offer

"IN MAY 1964, MY £1 BET PAID OFF WHEN WEST HAM BEAT PRESTON 3-2 IN THE FA CUP FINAL. THERE WAS QUITE A PARTY IN EAST LONDON, I CAN TELL YOU!"

The Oval in August 1947

I was a cricketer once…

IN 1956 my dad took me to Hesketh Park in Dartford to see Kent play Essex.

It was the home of Dartford Cricket Club and they had just built a new pavilion and increased the size of the outfield so this was by way of celebration. During the tea interval my dad spotted John Arlott walking across the pitch. "There you go Len, go and get his autograph." I ran over and asked him and do you know what he said? "Bugger off." But he said it so beautifully in that voice of his.

*John Arlott in the press box
at Lord's in 1980*

... but never a speedway rider!

THERE used to be many more speedway tracks in London and lots of teams.

Near me, there was the Hackney Hawks that started in 1963 at Hackney Wick Stadium but after 20 years they closed down. The West Ham Hammers finally closed down in 1971. And that's pretty much the story all over the capital.

Practising for the speedway World Team Championship at Wembley Stadium in September 1968. Great Britain had the world champion Ivan Mauger (left) in its team, together with another favourite, Martin Ashby

Hammers speedway supporters at Upton Park in 1947

~ DOWN THE ~

MARKET

~ SINCE 1944 ~

Markets were a part of my life from a very young age. They have been a major part of London life since the earliest times. They remind us that before supermarkets and even before there were shops in buildings people bought and sold from barrows and stalls in the open air. As time has gone on some people still like to do their shopping that way. There are also the huge indoor markets of Billingsgate, Covent Garden and Smithfield that have helped feed the capital for hundreds of years . . .

I GOT taken to markets from when I was very young, because my grandad was a real-life 'barrow boy', a costermonger, whose stall was on Bethnal Green Road. In the early days money was tight and so Grandad would pawn his gold watch every Monday morning for a couple of quid.

He would then go down to Spitalfields Market to buy whatever he could get. It was always cheap stuff – vegetables and fruit, but never of the best quality – he would load it on his barrow, a flat thing with two big wheels. They needed those barrows because all round Spitalfields Market there are cobbled streets and they were the only things that could be wheeled around easily.

Once he got his barrow back home, he sorted through what he'd managed to buy. Then he took his barrow to his pitch in Bethnal Green market where it turned into his stall – his was one of more than 200; for six days a week this was his routine.

"EVERY DAY ON THE WAY BACK FROM SPITALFIELDS, GRANDAD ALWAYS STOPPED AT A CAFÉ CALLED PELLICCI'S …WHENEVER I'M UP THAT WAY, I POP IN FOR A COFFEE AND TO REMINISCE"

By the end of the week he had made enough to keep things ticking over for another week, which meant giving my nan housekeeping money and Grandad Albert having enough to go down the pub. But not before he got his gold watch back so the whole routine could start again the following week.

To go to and from Spitalfields, Grandad would rope himself into his barrow, like a horse, and pull it the mile and half from Bethnal Green.

When I was about four or maybe five, just before I went to school, I would often go with him; it seemed like a real adventure to me.

He would put me on top of the barrow before pulling us back to his pitch in the market. Every day on the way back from Spitalfields, Grandad always stopped at a café called Pellicci's so he could have a cup of tea.

One day he bought a load of celery, which was verging on being rotten – costermongers called it 'melting', don't ask me why.

The celery always stuck in my mind because a few years later during the school holidays, when I was about 12, I was given the job of cleaning it.

First I had to put it into cold water to 'stiffen it up', then I'd clean it up by cutting off all the brown smelly leaves and then trim off any other rotten bits so we could sell it.

Pellicci's is still there. The café's interior is beautiful. The marquetry dates from the early 20th century – it's now a listed building; whenever I'm up that way I pop in for a coffee and to reminisce

Dawn start to fill the barrow

MY grandad took me to Spitalfields Market because it was the closest one to Bethnal Green from which to buy – Covent Garden was way too far for him to haul the barrow.

There had been a market at Spitalfields since 1638, although it did close down during the period when Oliver Cromwell was ruling England. It reopened in 1682 by order of Charles II in order to feed the growing population of this area of East London.

Today, Spitalfields is a very different kind of market and is housed in a purpose-built covered area originally built in 1887 and expanded in 1926.

Later, when my mum had her greengrocers shop in Falconwood Parade, Blackfen, and Grandad had progressed from a barrow to a shop on Bethnal Green Road, the family business bought a lorry – the horse had died.

My Uncle Albert and Aunt Ada still had a stall on Bethnal Green Road, while Grandad and Uncle George took care of the shop.

It was also Uncle George's job to go and buy the fruit and veg. In the 1950s, George would go up to Covent Garden Market at around four in the morning to buy the fruit and veg for all the two shops and the stall. He would then head south through the Blackwall Tunnel to deliver the first load to our shop in Blackfen and from there it was back up north to Bethnal Green by eight o'clock to drop off the rest.

This photo taken in 1948 is in Tavistock Street at the rear of Covent Garden Market. The market seen on the left of the picture was designed and built by Charles Fowler in 1830 and vacated in 1974 when the market moved to Nine Elms, south of the River Thames

SPITALFIELDS
LONDON
ENGLAND
MARKET
J. & E. PAGE Ltd
COVENT GARDEN

A Covent Garden wholesaler in 1955

"A MARKET PORTER CARRYING HIS BASKET IN THE TRADITIONAL WAY. I CANNOT HELP THINKING 'ELF AND SAFETY MIGHT HAVE SOMETHING TO SAY ABOUT THIS"

All these photos were taken in 1948, a time when congestion around Covent Garden was already reaching breaking point

From apples and pears to Apple computers

UNTIL the 16th century the area that is now called Covent Garden was arable land and orchards by Westminster Abbey; it was known as "the garden of the Abbey and Convent" and is first recorded as being referred to as Covent Garden in 1491. At the time of the Reformation, Henry VIII took the lands and gave them to the Earls of Bedford in 1552. It was the 4th Earl that commissioned Inigo Jones to build fine houses and along with it he built the Italianate arcaded square and the church of St Paul's.

Squares were a new concept for London and as such Covent Garden, as it was known, became a template for modern urban town planning. By 1654 a small open-air fruit and vegetable market was located on the south side of the fashionable square. Gradually, the whole area fell into disrepute, as taverns, theatres, coffeehouses and brothels opened up and by the 18th century it was a renowned red-light district.

Finally, Parliament acted and cleaned up the area and Charles Fowler's neo-classical building was erected in 1830 to cover and establish the market properly.

The market expanded to include the Floral Hall, Charter Market, and in 1904 the Jubilee Market but as it did so traffic congestion grew to the point where it was untenable to keep the produce market open any longer. In 1974 the market relocated to the New Covent Garden Market about three miles southwest at Nine Elms. The central building re-opened as a shopping centre in 1980 and is now a tourist attraction, which still includes market stalls nestling alongside the giant Apple computer store.

"THIS WAS JUST LIKE MY GRANDAD'S BARROW"

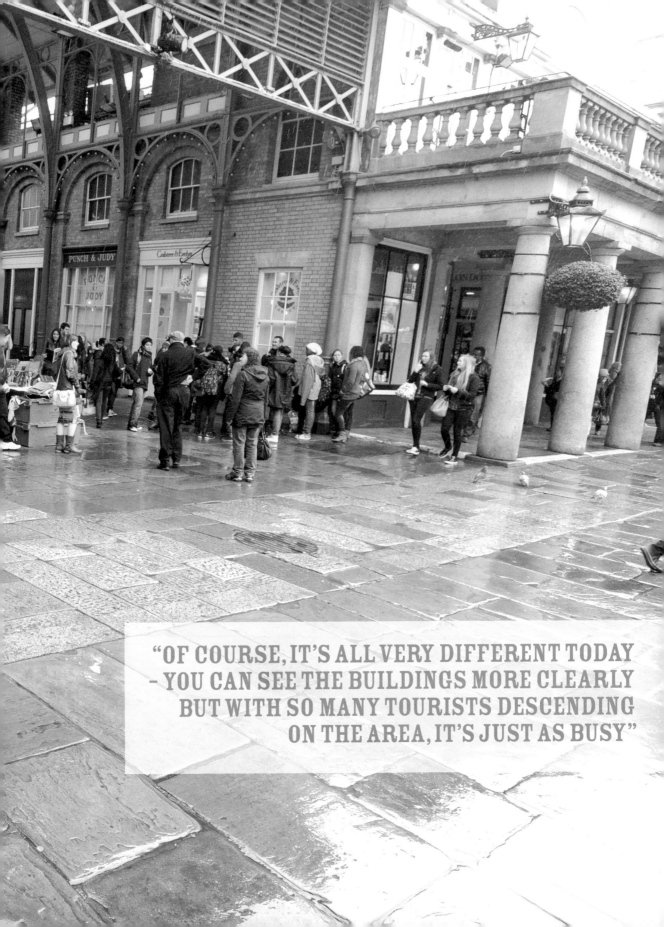

"OF COURSE, IT'S ALL VERY DIFFERENT TODAY – YOU CAN SEE THE BUILDINGS MORE CLEARLY BUT WITH SO MANY TOURISTS DESCENDING ON THE AREA, IT'S JUST AS BUSY"

My mum fell for the patter

THERE are numerous traditional markets located in London. Close to Spitalfields is Petticoat Lane Market which was not formally recognised until an Act of Parliament in 1936 but its long history as an informal shopping area makes it one of London's oldest surviving markets – its character is very different today than when I used to go there in the early 1960s.

When I was a boy, I went to Petticoat Lane with my mum to buy a wedding present for my auntie. There was a typical stallholder shouting about his wares: "I've got a dinner service, complete, not £20, not £15, not even £10, but £5, yes, only £5. Come on darling, I'm sure you'd like one."

Well my mum, who never ever fell for anything, fell for his patter. We paid the £5 and carried it home only to find when we opened it that all the crockery was odds and ends, nothing matched!

A silversmith's stall in Leather Lane in 1954

Leather Lane is another of London's very oldest street markets. It probably dates from the reign of Charles I but no-one is quite sure. It is still a market but has changed a lot in recent times and has struggled like other markets with access and parking and the congestion charges.

Back when the market was vibrant, serving both office workers at lunchtime and local residents in 1954

World on your doorstep

IN the 16th century, Whitechapel lay outside the city walls of London near to Aldgate.

Come 1840, and Whitechapel, along with Wapping, Aldgate, Bethnal Green, Mile End, Limehouse, Bow, Bromley-by-Bow, Poplar, Shadwell and Stepney, became what we have come to call the East End. Like every area it had its own market.

Back then people didn't travel far to either, work, shop or play.

By the Victorian era, Whitechapel had become a largely Jewish and Irish area of the East End.

During the war it was heavily damaged in the Blitz and many people moved out.

Today, Bangladeshis make up more than half the residents.

In Whitechapel Market, three years after I was born, the older character of the place was still in evidence. Today's market is mostly Asian and is another step along the evolutionary path of so much of this part of London

Today, Soho is a more sophisticated area of London with all kinds of trendy restaurants, bars and the like. And while it still has a character that is all its own it really was its own little enclave back in the middle part of the 20th century.

There are still a few market stalls in Soho but nothing like as busy as in these photographs. The colour pictures were taken in 1966 and are of Rupert Street which was the slightly more up-scale of the two Soho markets. The other, in Berwick Street, was further 'into' Soho and catered more to locals.

Rupert Street in 1955

*Berwick
Street Market
in 1963*

How much is that doggy in the basket?

THE market in Club Row between Spitalfields and Bethnal Green probably started in the late 17th century. When it became a purely pet market, no-one is quite sure.

When these photographs were taken in May 1946, the market was back in full swing after World War Two.

It was a Sunday-only market as it catered for people who were at work the rest of the week, unlike markets that sold foodstuffs that were required daily in the pre-refrigerator world.

Amid concerns about animal welfare the market was finally closed in 1983, 300 years after it first opened.

"I REMEMBER GOING TO THE CLUB ROW MARKET AS QUITE A SMALL CHILD. IN ITS EARLY DAYS, IT WAS THE PLACE IN LONDON TO BUY CAGED BIRDS, BUT AS TIME WENT ALONG, DOGS, CATS AND EVERY OTHER KIND OF DOMESTIC PET WAS FOR SALE"

The scene at Billingsgate Market on July 24, 1963

These fish porters were photographed in 1954 wearing their traditional hats that rank among the oddest to be found anywhere in the world. It's a type of flat-topped bowler with a turned up brim. Each hat is made from five pounds of leather, 400 brass rivets, and 30 feet of waxed thread. The porters carry boxes of wet fish on their heads and the brims are there to catch the drips

A fishy tale of foul language

IN the shadow of the Tower of London, in Lower Thames Street, Billingsgate Market took its name from Billingsgate Wharf, named after an ancient Britain.

By the 17th century, when an Act of Parliament established the market formally, it was also a byword for foul language!

By the early 19th century it was reported as a place that "did not bear frequent visits".

Prior to 1850, the market was a series of sheds that served as shelter for the fish sellers and fishmongers; the market was rebuilt to plans drawn up by J.B. Bunning, the architect to the City, in 1850.

Within a quarter of a century it had outgrown the space and the new architect, Sir Horace Jones, doubled the size of the market to 30,000 square feet, covering it with louver glass roofs, and adding a gallery for the sale of dried fish, with shellfish being served in the basement.

With the coming of the railways, fish no longer arrived at the wharf but instead came by train.

Like Covent Garden, the market outgrew its location. With the increasingly large vehicles used for transporting the fish, access was a major problem. In 1982, London's fish market relocated to a new 13-acre building complex on the Isle of Dogs, close to Canary Wharf in Docklands.

Above: In this 1966 photo the difficulty of access to Billingsgate Market is already becoming evident

Right: Like many London traders and businesses, cart horses were the way of transporting goods around the capital. These two were photographed at Billingsgate in 1954. When I was a small lad, my mates and I would scoop up the fresh horse-poo and then sell it for a 1d a bag to people that had gardens or window boxes and wanted some fertilizer!

Left: As with so many industries and businesses during World War Two, women came to play an increasingly important role on the Home Front. Here, in September 1943, a woman delivers boxes full of fish to traders at Billingsgate Market

The coster livin'

MY granddad was a costermonger. It is a word derived from old English, with 'coster' coming from Costard, meaning a type of apple and monger is a word for seller – it's a bit like fishmonger!

It was costermongers that sold in the markets and, in Victorian times through to the early part of the 20th century, they were the people that kept large parts of London fed. My granddad was definitely not a hawker – a hawker sells from a basket whereas a costermonger has a cart.

Since the 15th and 16th century, costermongers have been a major part of London life – Shakespeare for one mentions them.

By the mid 19th century, there were over 30,000 in London and it was at this time that they got a reputation for being among the less law-abiding citizens.

They developed their own language, were habitual swearers and were also competitive among themselves. To try to curb the rivalry between families and rival sellers, they developed the idea of having their own 'elders'; people that had the respect of the costermonger community. Out of this grew the idea of the Pearly Kings and Queens.

The Pearlies, as they are known, first began wearing clothes decorated with buttons in the mid-19th century when the costers were at their height. While traditional coster activity has died out, the Pearly Kings and Queens are alive and well, raising money for charities, as well as keeping the tradition alive.

These Pearly Kings and Queens were celebrating Covent Garden's 300th Birthday

This Costermongers Harvest Festival thanksgiving service was being held on October 3, 1954

"THE PEARLIES, AS THEY ARE KNOWN, FIRST BEGAN WEARING CLOTHES DECORATED WITH BUTTONS IN THE MID-19TH CENTURY WHEN THE COSTERS WERE AT THEIR HEIGHT"

Another scene from the thanksgiving service held on October 3, 1954

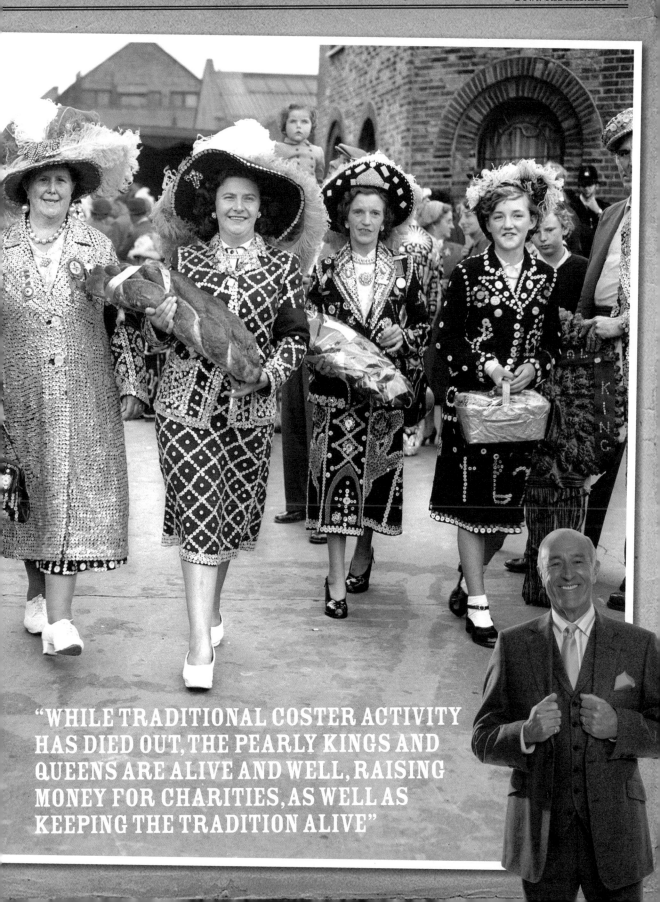

"WHILE TRADITIONAL COSTER ACTIVITY HAS DIED OUT, THE PEARLY KINGS AND QUEENS ARE ALIVE AND WELL, RAISING MONEY FOR CHARITIES, AS WELL AS KEEPING THE TRADITION ALIVE"

On the chopping block

SMITHFIELD was once fields, originally Smoothfields, and is located in the area of London that was originally called Farringdon Without.

There was also Farringdon Within, meaning one part was outside the city walls, the other within.

The meat market is the last surviving wholesale market in central London. It was also the place where executions of heretics and political opponents took place, including that of the Scottish patriot William Wallace.

Like Billingsgate, the imposing covered market was designed by Sir Horace Jones in the 19th century. Its history goes back to the 13th century when meat was first traded here. By 1726, Daniel Defoe said it was: "without question, the greatest in the world"; average yearly sales at Smithfield then were 74,000 cattle and 570,000 sheep. Two hundred years later and it was 220,000 head of cattle and 1,500,000 sheep.

This is Smithfield Market on July 6, 1954, on the day that meat rationing was finally ended after 14 years

In February 1936, 300 shop men decided to strike at Smithfield to secure a £4 minimum wage for a 40-hour week. It caused the shutdown of Smithfield, meaning that none of the usual 3,000 tonnes of meet was handled that day

"THE MEAT MARKET IS THE LAST SURVIVING WHOLESALE MARKET IN CENTRAL LONDON. ITS HISTORY GOES BACK TO THE 13TH CENTURY WHEN MEAT WAS FIRST TRADED HERE"

In 1945, a V-2 rocket struck at the north side of Charterhouse Street and caused massive damage to the market buildings.

Despite this, Smithfield is the only significant market that has not moved out of central London to expand or modernize its facilities, or being forced to do so for reasons of congestion.

Smithfield's buildings are on top of a warren of tunnels that were previously used as slaughterhouses and these, along with former railway tunnels, are now used for storage, parking and as basements.

Peel the other one

GRANDAD Albert was a smart bloke, a typical coster in that way. Take how he sold potatoes, maybe not the most glamorous of vegetables but he knew how to make a little extra on his sales.

He bought potatoes in 100 weight sacks and one day I watched how he would empty half of the potatoes from the sack into one bin and then the other half into the next-door bin.

He then reached over and took a card on which he wrote 'Selected – one penny & halfpenny/lb'. On the next-door bin containing potatoes from the same sack, he wrote 'Regular – one penny/lb'. I didn't understand this at all so I piped up: "Hang on, they're all from the same sack?" "Yes, my son, but you watch, the penny halfpenny ones will all go before the penny ones do; that's a little lesson you'll learn Lenny. If you under-sell yourself, people sort of don't respect you quite so much."

A more typical stall from the period

*The Caledonian Market near
Kings Cross is London's oldest
street market*

And he was right; all the more expensive ones went first. It was another great lesson.

It's what fascinated me about this photograph. It's from 1949 and apparently takings doubled when a deluxe street stall opened for business in London.

Instead of a wooden barrow with tarpaulin roof, housewives chose fruit and vegetables from metal shelves, had it weighed on built-in automatic scales and handed to them by assistants in white coats.

Sadly, it was not all good news and bad news was just around the corner. The stall was more than 2ft over the maximum permitted length of 9ft and the council insisted the size was reduced. Just goes to show that some things never change.

"GRANDAD ALBERT SOLD POTATOES, MAYBE NOT THE MOST GLAMOROUS OF VEGETABLES BUT HE KNEW HOW TO MAKE A LITTLE EXTRA ON HIS SALES..."

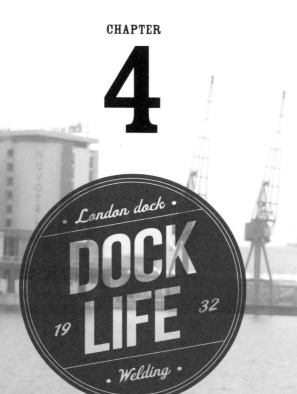

London's position is no accident.
The width of the Thames and the access
that the river offered to the North Sea
and the English Channel made the
siting of a port the key to ensuring that
London was a vibrant commercial city.
As ships became bigger, there was a
need to develop the docks and in 1815
the London Docks were built. As a
young welder, I got a job repairing ships
in the docks and being close to the River
Thames is still something I love . . .

Being a welder, I never considered myself a docker but believe you me, most of the people I worked with looked like this when they turned up for work. This photo from 1965 shows dockers awaiting the daily allocation of work

Clocking up a few extra shillings

THE Port of London was once the largest in the world. London's Docks grew out of the fact that the port, along the Thames embankment, simply ran out of capacity.

Throughout the 19th century, a series of enclosed dock systems was built, starting with West India Docks (1802), East India Docks (1803), London Docks (1805), Surrey Commercial Docks (1807), St Katharine Docks (1828), Royal Victoria Dock (1855), Millwall Dock (1868), Royal Albert Dock (1880), and finally Tilbury Docks (1886). The Royal Victoria Dock was the biggest of all the London docks in the first half of the 20th century.

In the early part of the 20th century the Port of London Authority was established to more effectively run the whole of

> ## "IT WAS AMAZING HOW MANY JOBS FINISHED AT 5.15 – AN EXTRA 15 MINUTES WORK FOR WHICH WE WERE PAID TWO HOURS"

the docks. Prior to the war, 60 million tonnes was going through the PLA docks but during wartime this was largely switched to Glasgow and Liverpool. By 1960s the figure was back to 60 million tonnes but by this time much of it was moving through Tilbury, and that became even more significant after most of docks upstream near London closed in the late 1960s and the Tilbury Container port opened in the 1970 at Northfleet Hope.

When the docks all finally closed in the 1970s, the borough of Tower Hamlets took over the eight square miles of docks and filled in some large areas of the Western docks with the idea of building houses on the land.

This never happened and in 1981 the London Docklands Development Corporation acquired the land and set about developing the area into what today is one of the most vibrant parts of the capital.

I worked in the docks at the start of the 1960s at Harland and Wolff at the Royal Docks in North Woolwich. I worked on ship repairs and, prior to me working there and welding being the method of repair, there were four-man gangs that did the riveting.

With the advent of welding Harland and Wolff thought they could get away with using a two-man crew, naturally the unions disagreed and after a dispute the gangs stayed as a four-man team. This meant that for every single electric arc welding gun there were two welders, so when one of you was welding the other one wouldn't be welding.

To operate the machine that created the electricity to drive the welding gun it needed a man to look after it; this was the plant minder. He sat on his bum all day long and the fourth guy became the fire guy in case of any incidents occurring.

It was a bit like that film starring Peter Sellers, 'I'm Alright Jack', in which Peter plays a union official who refuses to co-operate with management. Harland and Wolff was keen to get ships in and out of the dock as fast as it could.

In reality, if a job went on after 5pm, our normal knocking-off time, we were paid up until 7pm. It was amazing just how many jobs actually finished at 5.15. an extra 15 minutes work for which we were paid two hours.

Similarly on bigger projects, where we had to go past 7pm it meant that we were paid until 9pm, once again a lot of jobs finished at a quarter past seven.

The real big bonus was when things went on until after 9pm, that would mean you were paid right around until the next morning – no matter what time you clocked off.

To look at the docks in 1951 (left), you wouldn't have thought back then that people would one day be living in trendy flats on what was a massive, thriving site

*Victoria Docks
pool in November
1964*

*Strike-bound ships in October 1954 during
one of the strikes at London Docks*

In 1965 the Port of London Authority employed dock guides to show people around the docks; sadly it was a short-lived move

The docks empty of shipping in the 1970s shortly before being taken over by the London Docklands Development Corporation

Captain Scott aboard his ship, the Terra Nova, before setting off on his ill-fated journey to the South Pole. Scott set out on June 1,1910, from the East India Dock, close to where the Canary Wharf development now stands

The passenger ferry Catherine at East India Docks in 1935. East India Docks was the first of London's docks to close, in 1967. Today, the area is largely a residential development

Canary Wharf and the Docklands today

"IN 1981, THE LONDON DOCKLANDS DEVELOPMENT CORPORATION ACQUIRED THE LAND AND SET ABOUT DEVELOPING THE AREA INTO WHAT TODAY IS ONE OF THE MOST VIBRANT PARTS OF THE CAPITAL"

CHAPTER

5

That's Entertainment

~ LONDON ~

When I was growing up, entertainment consisted of going to the pictures, seeing the occasional group or singer or going dancing. Even television wasn't much of an option, as it was all black and white and there wasn't much of it! Entertainment was usually found closer to home and while I did start venturing into the West End in the 1960s it was only for a big night out or to go dancing. Every part of London had several cinemas and places to go dancing and generally speaking it was a simpler time . . .

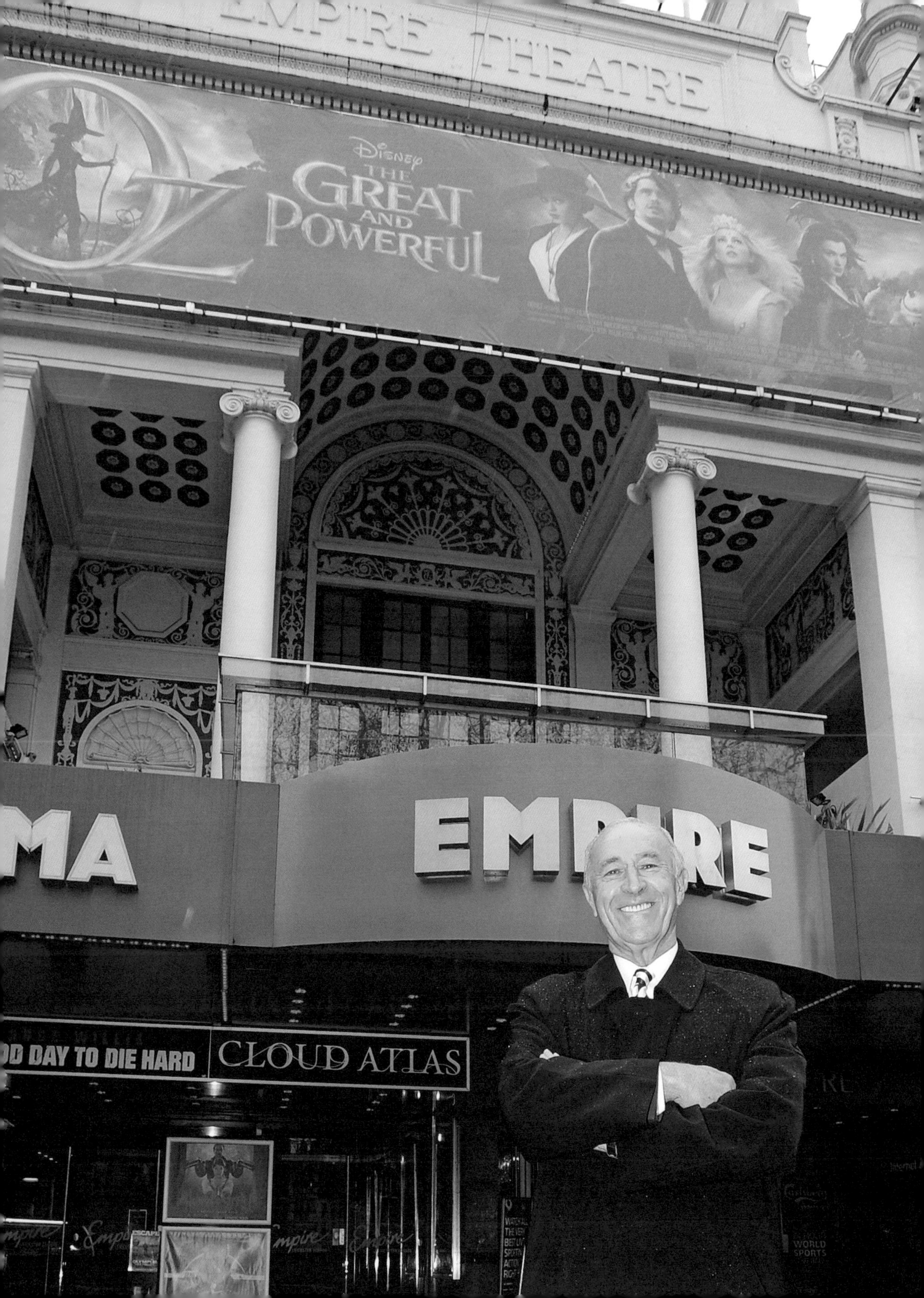
EMPIRE THEATRE
DISNEY
THE GREAT AND POWERFUL
MA
EMPIRE
OD DAY TO DIE HARD
CLOUD ATLAS

ASIDE from making our own entertainment, I think, like many people my age – and even quite a bit younger – my first exposure to the entertainment industry was going to see a film, going to the pictures. When I was a boy, maybe 11 or thereabouts, and wanted to go into a film, one to which you had to be accompanied by an adult, we would stand outside the picture house and ask a man to take us in.

"Mister, will you take us in mister. We won't sit with you, promise." This was especially important if he was with his bird. It was an altogether more innocent age.

Later on, I was the one going to see a film with a girl and that first time was a bit of an ordeal. Her name was Sally and she and I went to the Granada in Welling in Kent to see the 4pm double feature that finished at 7pm, giving me enough time to get Sally home by 7.30pm. In the flicks we sat side by side watching the film, neither of us moving. Now you'll have to trust me when I tell you that I'm not sure how this happened but suddenly we were holding hands. It was magic.

It must have been hot in the pictures, either that or nerves were playing a part, because both our hands were both wringing wet with sweat by the end of the first film.

During the interval I nipped down the front, because we were naturally sat at the back in the stalls, to where the usherette was selling ice creams and bought us a tub of Wall's vanilla ice cream. I hated the taste of the lid, having licked it once, and thereafter always thought people that licked the lid of a tub were a bit odd. Sally didn't lick hers.

The second film was barely past the opening credits when I put my arm around Sally and her head rested on my shoulder. It was like Antony and Cleopatra. There was only one problem, her hair was so highly lacquered it was like having a Brillo pad rubbing against my face. That and the fact that it smelled; it was like sniffing glue, which I think added to feeling as though I was getting high. I thought that going to the pictures with a girl was the best thing that had ever happened to me in my life.

> **"IN THE FLICKS WE SAT SIDE BY SIDE WATCHING THE FILM, NEITHER OF US MOVING ... I'M NOT SURE HOW THIS HAPPENED BUT SUDDENLY WE WERE HOLDING HANDS. IT WAS MAGIC"**

By the spring of 1962 I was going out with a girl that I had met at dancing at the Embassy – she was a really good dancer. One night I asked her if she'd like to go to the pictures during the week. She wanted to go and see West Side Story and as I, even then, loved musicals I readily agreed.

From the opening sequence, which features the Sharks and the Jets, I was hooked and have continued to be. Nothing could compare with the dancing in that film, for me it's one of the greatest films of all time and I've watched it umpteen times. I loved the songs too, 'Somewhere', 'Something's Coming', 'Tonight', 'Maria', and 'America' take me back to that first time I saw the film at the Granada in Welling.

The place to meet girls

FOR me growing up, entertainment consisted of first the Boys' Brigade, then the Sea Cadets and finally the Boy Scouts, although that didn't last too long because I was no good at knottery!

Then as a teenager I graduated to the youth club at Falconwood Parade. Back then, before kids had money, mobile phones, iPods and all the other stuff of our ever upwardly mobile society, the youth club was the place to go to meet girls.

It was soft drinks, music on the Dansette record player and maybe even a visit from the vicar in whose church hall the youth club was often held.

Sometimes there was even a local band . . .

Johnny and the Thunderclaps play at their local youth club in 1960. Whatever happened to them?

Teenagers crowd around the tape and record player at their youth club in 1961

Two teenage boys playing dominoes at Blackheath youth club in March 1959. Blackheath was just up the road from me but you only ever went to your local club

The tragedy at the Café de Paris

THE Café de Paris, close to London's Leicester Square, opened in 1924 and by the 1930s was a fashionable nightclub frequented by the rich and famous – even the Prince of Wales was a regular visitor.

During the war the club was packed most nights of the week and despite air raid warnings the band just kept on playing. However, in March 1941, two landmines devastated the Café de Paris. When I was putting this book together The Mirror showed me their report of the terrible events that for censorship reasons did not reveal the exact location.

A packed dance hall was wrecked, and a bus and a row of shops and offices were demolished when bombs fell in a London area on Saturday night. Several people in the dance hall were killed, and others were so injured that they died in hospital. At least half the people in the fully occupied bus, and people sheltering in neighbouring doorways, were killed. Sixty couples – munitions workers, soldiers on leave and typists – were on the dance floor when four H.E. bombs whistled down. One hit the dance hall, blowing out one end of it. The lights crashed down. Dancers were flung to the floor. Debris cascaded on young couples.

More than 30 people died and around 60 were injured at the Café de Paris, including the West Indian bandleader, Ken 'Snakehips' Johnson. Johnson was dead but with no signs of injury, with a flower in his buttonhole. He was 26 years old. After I took up ballroom dancing, I danced there many times and it was later that I found out the story of the tragedy.

"AFTER I TOOK UP BALLROOM DANCING, I DANCED THERE MANY TIMES AND IT WAS LATER THAT I FOUND OUT THE STORY OF THE TRAGEDY"

The entrance to Café de Paris in November 1950, two years after it reopened. Commissionaires and doormen in pukka uniforms is another thing you don't see these days

Clearly visible in the aftermath of the bombing is Joey Deniz's guitar. The guitarist, although injured, survived the blast

"CLUBS IN LONDON WERE AT THEIR MOST SOPHISTICATED IN THE THIRTIES. AFTER THE POST-WAR HARDSHIPS THEY BEGAN TO PICK UP AGAIN IN THE SIXTIES BUT WERE MOSTLY OUT OF REACH FOR THE LIKES OF ORDINARY PEOPLE"

Neon comes to town

WHEN I was old enough to go to clubs, they were certainly not the sophisticated places found in the West End. Clubs in London were at their most sophisticated in the 1930s and after the post-war hardships they began to pick up again in the 1960s but were mostly out of reach for the likes of ordinary people.

Take George Raft's Colony Club in London's Berkley Square. Raft was an actor who starred in a number of 1940s films, often portraying a gangster. By the 1950s his career had stalled and he was reduced to mixing with gangsters in real life, as he had become a part owner of a Mafia-run casino in pre-Castro Cuba.

With the demise of Mafia activities in Havana in 1959 when Castro came to power the Mafia's attention switched to other opportunities, including London, where gambling had been legalised. The Colony Club opened in London and was operated by American Cosa Nostra mobsters Meyer Lansky and Angelo Bruno.

However, by 1967, the police had begun investigating the Colony club and several Cosa Nostra mobsters were deported and George Raft was refused entry into the UK for his mob connections. Raft died in 1980, aged 79.

The Colony Club in 1967

These London nightclubs, pictured in 1960, give a hint of how different it was. The idea of an 'American' bar sounded exotic and the use of neon lighting was only really becoming more widespread in London

Dad took me to see Pops

IN May 1956, my dad took me to see Louis Armstrong at the vast Empress Hall in Lillie Road, Earls Court, on his first visit to Britain since the 1930s.

At the time, for some reason, I thought I was going to see Fats Waller, although he had been dead for over a decade. Anyway, we were there along with 5,000 other fans of a man who was a towering legend in jazz. At one point my dad whispered in my ear: "Len, see who's sitting next to you?"

I looked and was none the wise. "It's Joe Davis, the snooker player, he was a world champion," he whispered.

I loved the music and still do love Louis Armstrong's playing and singing. It was reported later that Princess Margaret went to see him and then, on the last night, Humphrey Littleton, whose band had opened for Satchmo, put a crown on Armstrong's head, pronouncing him 'The King of Jazz'.

Louis Armstrong shakes hands with trombonist Trummy Young and, in the other photograph, from left, Trummy Young, Louis Armstrong, Barrett Deems on drums, clarinetist Edmond Hall and Arvell Shaw on bass

First time I heard the Beatles

BY 1963, I had become a Mod, but more about that later...

We would take frequent trips down to Brighton to our 'base' at the Skylark a pub just off the beach. It was in the Skylark that I first heard the Beatles on the jukebox; it stopped me in my tracks.

From that day on I became a fan, although I never did get to see them, despite them playing the Granada Cinema in East Ham in November 1963. It was on this, their first headlining tour of the UK, that Beatlemania officially began. A Daily Mirror journalist, who was attempting to put into words the scenes he witnessed on the first night of their five-week tour at the Odeon Cinema in sleepy, conservative Cheltenham, coined the term. From then on it just got crazier! I did get to Buddy Holly at the Granada Woolwich, Ray Charles at the Gaumont Lewisham, Cliff Richard and Marty Wilde at the Granada Dartford.

Do you remember doing this? Going down the record shop asking them to play you the latest record by your favourite artist

Paul and Linda McCartney at a Buddy Holly party in London in 1982

Ray Charles with writer Raina Johnson around the time I saw him in 1963

Exterior view of the Windmill Theatre in 1958

"THE WINDMILL THEATRE IN THE HEART OF SOHO BOASTED THAT 'WE NEVER CLOSED' AND THEIR 'TASTEFUL' NUDE SHOWS ATTRACTED NOT JUST SERVICEMEN IN LONDON ON LEAVE, BUT PEOPLE FROM ALL WALKS OF LIFE – THEIR SLOGAN WAS PARODIED AS 'WE'RE NEVER CLOTHED'"

Bombs or no bombs – the show goes on

DURING World War Two, the need for entertainment was so important. There was a need to relieve the stress and despite tragedies like the Café De Paris and other ballrooms that were bombed during the Blitz, it did not stop people going out.

People grabbed any and every opportunity to visit the cinema, the theatre and dances. The Windmill Theatre in the heart of Soho boasted that 'we never closed' and their 'tasteful' nude shows attracted not just servicemen in London on leave but people from all walks of life; their slogan was parodied as "we're never clothed". Laura Henderson had originally bought the theatre in the early 1930s and had it remodelled into a small auditorium but it proved unprofitable and it returned to showing films.

It returned to being a theatre after Vivian van Damm was hired as manager and in 1932 she came up with the idea of a Revudeville, a non-stop programme of vaudeville that ran from the early afternoon until 11pm. It featured dancers and showgirls but this too proved to be unprofitable until van Damm came up with the idea of having nude girls similar to those featured at the Moulin Rouge and Folies Bergères in Paris. The only problem was they were forbidden from moving – if there was even the slightest twitch they risked the censors closing the theatre.

Apart from the 12 days at the very start of the war, when theatres across London were compulsorily closed, the Windmill stayed open throughout the war; the cast sheltered in the two underground floors during the worst days of the Blitz.

These days the Windmill still offers a racy style of entertainment.

The owner of the Windmill Theatre, Laura Henderson, seen here in 1943 during a break in rehearsals

Free entertainment on your own estate

IN the early 1950s we didn't get to go on holiday too much and nor did too many people who grew up in London during those post-war years.

It was a very different world back then. I found this amazing photo looking through the archive of The Mirror newspaper. It turns out that Westminster City Council decided to send a show featuring dancers, clowns and jugglers around their various housing estates. This was taken at Queen Mary's Buildings, Stillington Street, and shows more than 1,000 children watching in July 1953.

It was a free show, happy days!

CHAPTER

6

Seven! How come a bloke like me
suddenly ended up on the TV judging a
ballroom dancing competition? Well, as
you might know by now I've spent most
of my working life involved in dancing,
as a competitor, teacher and judge. I love
dancing, all kinds of it and when I was a
teenager it was as though there was a new
dance being invented every week . . .

A date with destiny

MY father met Mum at a dance in the 1930s; it's where so many young couples met for the two decades each side of World War Two. By the time I was 14, some of my mates from school started going to the Court School of Dancing in Welling.

I tagged along one night but the only trouble was I only vaguely knew how to quickstep, so I had to keep sitting out the dances until one came along. As the weeks went by, I got to grips with more dances, including the basics of the Waltz, the Foxtrot, the cha-cha-cha and the Jive. Soon, I was asking more girls to dance and I discovered a substitute for conkers, dinky toys and marbles.

Come the early Sixties I wanted to spend less time at places like the Court School of Dancing, I wanted to rock and roll. But my dad never gave up on me when it came to try to get me into ballroom dancing. It was after my footballing injury that I really got into ballroom dancing and after that I never looked back. I graduated to the Erith Dance Studio that was on two floors right above Burton's, the gentleman's tailor. Our classes were on the first floor and on the floor above that was where Henry Kingston used to teach. I say teach but in actual fact he was a coach, not a teacher. In dancing a coach is well above a teacher, neither was he just any old coach, but a top coach. Henry and Joy Tolhurst had been dance partners and were also married. They had been one of the top couples in the dance world for many years but Henry was an even better coach than he was a dancer.

They saw something in me and I ended up dancing in competitions, at first all over London and then pretty soon I was dancing in competitions all around the country. After Henry Kingston passed away in the mid-1960s I started to teach at The Erith Dance Studio, which meant I also gave up my job in the docks and with it my dancing life truly began. While I am the first to admit that I was never a great dancer, I was not world-class, I certainly found my vocation when it came to teaching. In the early 1970s I opened the Len Goodman Dance Centre in Dartford – I had achieved my destiny, I was a dance teacher in Dartford.

Little did I know what all that was going to lead to…

Come Dancing was first on our TV screens in 1949 and stayed there until 1998. Victor Sylvester hosted Dancing Club on the TV for 17 years and these two shows commanded a huge audience in their heyday. It was in 2004 that Strictly Come Dancing debuted on the TV and I had the biggest break of my whole life

"WHILE I AM THE FIRST TO ADMIT
I WAS NEVER A GREAT DANCER, I
CERTAINLY FOUND MY VOCATION
WHEN IT CAME TO TEACHING"

Those Jiving, Jitterbugging, Bunny-Hopping, Strolling Fifties...

THE 1950s really was the start of the era of the dance craze. It seemed like there was a new one every week. There was the Madison, it started in Columbus Ohio in the late 1950s and soon spread to Britain. Back in 1952 the Bunny Hop started in San Francisco and then there was the Stroll, the Hand Jive and of course jiving itself. In truth the Jive started in the 1930s with Cab Calloway but with the coming of rock 'n' roll in the Fifties it took on a whole new importance. In Britain it was American soldiers that brought over Jitterbugging and the Lindy Hop, which did so much to influence the Jive.

Hand jiving in November 1956 in a London club

In 1949 barefoot dancing was banned for some reason but it certainly didn't stop these dancers at The Paramount in London's Tottenham Court Road

Dancing at a jazz club to a live band in January 1955

This was a more formal Jive Championship at a Haringey dance hall in June 1956

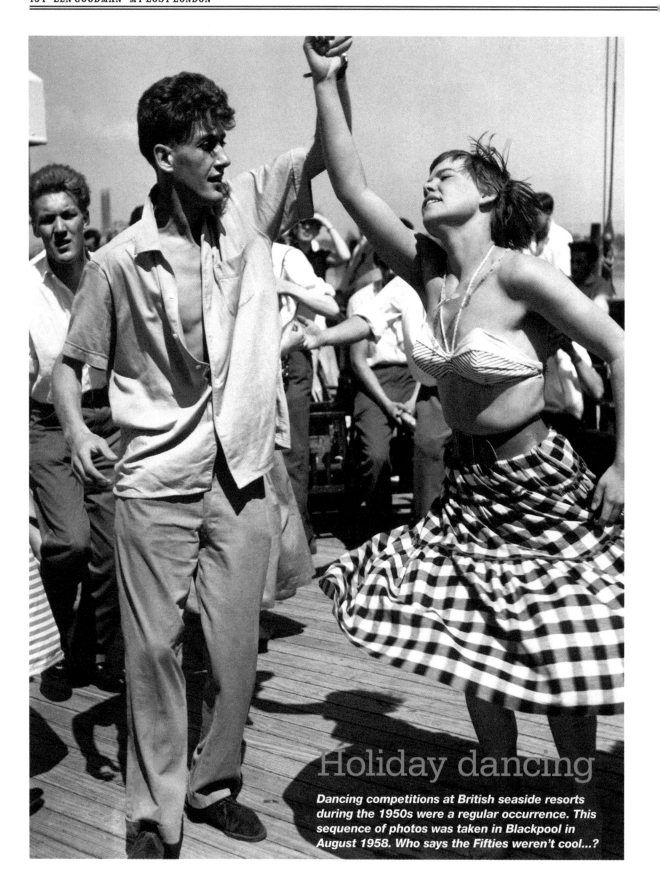

Holiday dancing

Dancing competitions at British seaside resorts during the 1950s were a regular occurrence. This sequence of photos was taken in Blackpool in August 1958. Who says the Fifties weren't cool...?

It was all part of the Daily Mirror's Blackpool Week with Bill Gregory's band

In 1952, Sugar Ray Robinson retired from boxing having won 131 out of 136 of his fights. He briefly became a dancer and said the training was harder than when he was a boxer. He's seen here entertaining at a showbusiness party in London in April 1956. He had already gone back to boxing by this time and regained the middleweight crown. It's interesting that none of the boxers on Strictly or Dancing With The Stars have ever been any good at dancing. Sugar Ray Leonard, who appeared on the American series, gave me a signed boxing glove because he said I'd been nice to him!

"SUGAR RAY LEONARD, WHO APPEARED ON THE AMERICAN SERIES, GAVE ME A SIGNED BOXING GLOVE BECAUSE HE SAID I'D BEEN NICE TO HIM!"

Dancing takes a twist

IN the 1960s, along came a whole new series of dance crazes, led of course by the Twist, a dance still performed by many men at wedding receptions and any other event where dads are required to dance.

A change that had begun in the 1950s continued to gather pace as the 1960s came along. First, the jukebox began replacing bands to dance to and then discotheques began to spring up. One reason was the technology in amplification allowed for records to be used; previously, a band had been the only way to fill a dance hall with music. To tell you the truth, one of the things I most enjoy about Strictly is the live band. They do a fantastic job and it's a pleasure to hear top professionals doing their stuff.

The Twist arrived in London from America in 1961 and these dancers are demonstrating it to diners at the Satire Club on Duke of York Street, London, in October

"ONE OF THE THINGS I MOST ENJOY ABOUT STRICTLY IS THE LIVE BAND"

Even after the demise of the big band after World War Two there were still plenty of opportunities for live musicians at many clubs and dance halls in and around London. This band is playing for the couple demonstrating the Twist

The Café de Paris has seen just about every style of dancing there is come and go. Here, Lionel Blair demonstrates the NEW Madison in September 1962

Ready Steady Go! was the epitome of the Swinging Sixties and was first broadcast in August 1963 from TV House in London's Kingsway. Broadcasting on a Friday evening with its slogan 'The Weekend Starts Here', it became synonymous with the era. RSG! was Britain's weekly look at the 'fab, happening scene' in London. As well as the bands it showed the dancers and did much to promote the latest dance fads. Our photo was taken in February 1964

This dance came and went without me noticing it! Young Mods, hands clasped behind their backs like Prince Philip, dance the blues in Basildon, Essex, in September 1963. The band is The Dave Clark Five

The jukebox changed so much in America and they soon spread to Britain. No self-respecting club or coffee bar owner would be without one

Most weekday nights I would be in Lorraine's Coffee bar in Welling, drinking a frothy coffee, or sometimes at the Embassy or the Savoy in Catford, which was another dance hall I used to frequent. It wasn't long before I started going up to London with some of my mates. Sunday's was a favourite for going up town because they had an afternoon dance at the Lyceum in the Strand. This couple is competing in the Twist and Beat Championships of Great Britain at the Lyceum in December 1965

Down the Palais

DANCING is probably man's earliest form of entertainment and whereas in the recent past teenagers and the young went to discos or went clubbing, ballroom dancing had been a hugely popular pursuit.

From the 1930s through to the 1960s, many more people went dancing on a regular basis; there were far less choices of alternate forms of entertainment.

It was the same with football; more people went to watch football on a Saturday in the 1930s than they do now. In those days, every town, every village, every church hall had dancing going on. In London and the big cities there were huge places to go dancing, including the Hammersmith Palais, the Locarno in Streatham and the Royal in Tottenham, where thousands danced nearly every night of the week. Take Hammersmith Palais, which recently closed down, it, was a huge draw for dancers and in its heyday it could accommodate several thousand on the dance floor.

The Hammersmith Palais in the 1960s

"IN LONDON AND THE BIG CITIES THERE WERE HUGE PLACES TO GO DANCING, INCLUDING THE HAMMERSMITH PALAIS, THE LOCARNO AND THE ROYAL IN TOTTENHAM"

The Empire Cinema at Leicester Square in June 1963

An old favourite that's still standing

THE Rivoli is London's only remaining original 1950s ballroom and I danced there hundreds of times over the years. It's beautiful interior has featured in films, video shoots and in more recent times rock bands have also used it for concerts. It was originally a cinema and was converted to a dance hall in the late 1950s.

The owners of the Ballroom in 2008, Ben and Jeannie Mannix

It features a second function room with a ceiling covered with photographs of Old Master paintings (left)

Either side of the ballroom are two bars, running the length of the hall. The right-hand bar built in 1958 (right) features booths and tables with leather upholstery arranged like a railway carriage

CHAPTER

THE WAY
WE LIVED
THEN

The way we lived was not better or worse
than the way we live now – it was just
different. Communications in all its forms
have probably been one of the things that
have changed the world the most. Whether
it's through the use of mobile telephones
and the internet, right down to television
and radio – remember, radios were not
fitted in most cars until the 1960s and then
they were mostly AM radios that meant
that music was hard to listen to . . .

THERE's a price to be paid for progress. It means that some of the things that you really enjoyed about your earlier life get lost as new things take over.

Of course, none of us can do anything to stop change happening, we just go with the flow. Having said that, I think there are many things about modern life that are way better than the old days.

Take the infamous London smog. It killed thousands of people and made life so miserable for hundreds of thousands more.

I remember once in the 1950s being with my dad in the car, when the fog was so bad we had to pull over and stop because he could no longer even see the curb. We sat there until a bus came along and then we joined the procession of cars following the bus.

The reason the bus was able to navigate was because the bus conductor walked in front of the bus. Of course most buses don't even have a conductor these days, having just a driver and the Oyster Card reader.

Technology has made some jobs redundant as well as creating jobs too. For every chimney sweep employed in London during the post-war years there are probably the equivalent number of people working in shops selling mobile phones! Some tradesmen, like rag and bone men, have to some extent been replaced by the council tip and the charity shop; there was no need for charity shops when I was growing up as people didn't have enough to get rid of, and what they had they recycled in some way.

When we moved from the East End to Kent in the mid-1950s we got a nice new house but it still had no central heating, it was just open fires downstairs.

Getting ready for bed in the winter was a speedy activity. In the coldest weather I used to get dressed and undressed in bed; I would have all my school clothes by the side of the bed. My rule was a simple one. When Mum woke me up to go to school and I could see my breath, then I got dressed under the covers.

Add to all that the way we shop, go on holiday and use our leisure time and it was a vastly different world in London during the post-war years.

The view of Trafalgar Square and London even as recently as 1963 shows how very different it all was. Very few high-rise buildings and you could drive all the way around the square

The old pea soupers

THE infamous London pea souper was not so much fog as smog. The often yellowish smog was caused by air pollution containing soot particulates and the poisonous gas sulphur dioxide.

During Victorian times and the early part of the 20th century, these were not at all uncommon with the increasing industrialisation in the Thames Valley and London. Nearly everyone used coal fires to heat their homes and in larger houses there were fires in a number of rooms.

Eventually, this led to the Clean Air Act 1956, which banned the use of coal for domestic fires in urban areas. It was revised in 1968 when the Act made it illegal for industries burning coal, gas or other fuels to use anything but tall chimneys.

The worst recorded instance of a pea souper in my lifetime was the Great Smog of 1952, when 4,000 deaths were reported in London in just a couple of days. Recent estimates have revised this upwards to around 12,000.

It occurred in December when there were many more fires alight than normal during a period when it was even colder than usual. Added to which, on the evening of December 5, there was an anticyclone that made the air very still, as well as warm, which prevented the colder air and the smoke from dispersing. As more fires were burning there was a build up at ground level that created these freak conditions.

On the first day of the smog, visibility dropped to a few yards and two days later it was down to one foot.

It became impossible for cars to move and motorists simply abandoned them, which meant ambulances could not reach people affected by the smog, pushing up the death toll. Those that were treated had usually walked to hospital, many with blue lips from the effects of the suffocating smog.

My dad and me had been to see his mum on the first day of the 1952 smog and when we had left home it was already getting thick. When we left my nan's house to walk home it was incredible, in fact if you did not live through this it's almost impossible to imagine it's true. It was a half-mile walk back to our place and we couldn't find our way home. We walked the route, which we had walked many times and were completely lost. Eventually, we found a street sign and went right up to it to read it and found we had gone past our street. We retraced our steps and eventually got home and then never went out again until after the smog cleared a few days later.

Chimneys of an East End factory poke through the blanket of smog covering London in 1952

"THE WORST RECORDED INSTANCE OF A PEA SOUPER IN MY LIFETIME WAS THE GREAT SMOG OF 1952, WHEN 4,000 DEATHS WERE REPORTED IN LONDON IN JUST A COUPLE OF DAYS"

Scenes from London's smog

PEA soupers have had many mentions in literature and were often a feature of American films when they wanted to portray London.

In Charles Dickens' Bleak House, when Esther arrives in London, she asks: "Whether there was a great fire anywhere? For the streets were so full of dense brown smoke that scarcely anything was to be seen. 'Oh, dear no, miss,' he said. 'This is a London particular.' I had never heard of such a thing. 'A fog, miss,' said the young gentleman."

Contrary to popular belief, smog and fog are not that prevalent in the writings of Sir Arthur Conan Doyle in his Sherlock Holmes stories. A Study in Scarlet written in 1887 makes reference to "a dun-coloured veil hung over the housetops."

Even after the Clean Air Act, smog continued to be a problem before the amendment to the act dealing with industrial chimneys was introduced. These two photos show people wearing smog masks in December 1962

Smog Wardens in action in January 1956

Battersea Power Station, November 1949

Even after the smog was beginning to lift, it was still very difficult to get around. This policeman on point duty was using flares to guide the traffic on December 8, 1952

A policeman picked out by searchlights directing traffic in the fog and dark of a late autumn evening in October 1958

A London bus in the fog, November 1949

Crowds stuck at Waterloo station as trains are delayed due to smog in December 1962

Bobbies on bicycles

DO you remember the old Roger Miller song called 'England Swings'? In it he paints a picture of what London was like in the Swinging Sixties, and it was typical of the way that many Americans saw the way we lived during the decade when British bands took the music of Liverpool and London to America.

It was helped, just like the enduring image of the London fog, by constant references by American TV shows and movies that were usually filmed somewhere in Hollywood, pretending to be London.

They really did think that bobbies rode around on bikes but in truth most policemen walked the beat. Of course, it's something we still talk about today. "Not enough police on foot" is an often-heard complaint.

There was one reason particular reason why the police walked the beat. In those pre-mobile phone and sophisticated communications days getting policemen to where things were happening was a difficult task. Added to which there were many more policemen doing traffic duty than there are today.

Recently, I thought to myself, I wonder how many more sets of traffic lights there are in London? The answer is a staggering 6,000 sets, which if only one in 10 had a policeman on duty previously, that's an awful lot of policeman. I'd love to know how many more there are than back in the 1950s.

To communicate, police had telephone call boxes – not all of them were like the one in Dr Who

Did you know that the first person convicted of speeding in the UK was Walter Arnold of East Peckham, Kent, just up the road from where I lived? It was in January 1896 and he was caught doing 8 mph when the speed limit was 2 mph; he was fined one shilling plus costs. It would have been quicker to walk. The Metropolitan Police conducted this early experiment with a radar trap on the Thames Embankment in January 1958

Charing Cross station and The Strand in August 1969 shows clearly the lack of traffic lights and a policeman directing traffic. Just how many policeman were involved in this activity day-to-day is impossible to calculate

Keeping London moving

The reason there are many more cyclists in this scene is that it was taken during the General Strike in May 1926

Directing traffic in the late 1930s

Bond Street in October 1947

*Wellington Street, Covent Garden
in October 1947*

Do people still ask a policeman for directions? This was in February 1953

Swinging London

THE epitome of 'Swinging London' was Carnaby Street. While I bought most of my clothes locally, I started to venture into London and particularly Carnaby Street around the mid-1960s. Levis were £1 19s and 11d and they were not sold pre-shrunk, so you had to put them on and sit in the bath until they had. It was a devil's own job to get rid of all the blue dye!

John Stephen, the self-proclaimed King of Carnaby Street, opened the first of his shops, 'His Clothes' in 1963. He was soon followed by I Was Lord Kitchener's Valet, Lady Jane, Kleptomania, Mates, Ravel and a string of others who all catered for pop stars and young people who wanted to look like pop stars.

From everyone dressing the same, everyone wanted to dress differently and designers like Mary Quant, Lord John, Merc and Irvine Sellars were on hand to create the fashions that allowed us all to 'express ourselves'. Carnaby Street became a Mecca for London's "mod" followers, and before long the entire street was full of trendy boutiques. This was Carnaby Street in 1965.

"CARNABY STREET BECAME A MECCA FOR LONDON'S 'MOD' FOLLOWERS AND BEFORE LONG IT WAS FULL OF TRENDY BOUTIQUES"

The Bank of England around 1903

City slickers

THE total opposite from the fashions of the 1960s and, ever since, was always the City of London.

Men dressed conservatively, almost in the uniform of their particular trade. These days that's all changed too when people have a much more relaxed dress code even when working in the City.

In 1959 this city type was the epitome of what people thought of as a city gent with his rolled umbrella

A banker in the City of London in 1963

Barristers crossing the road outside the Royal Courts of Justice in 1948

Technological casualties

THERE are so many things that you do not see around London any longer that are as a result of changing technology. While we are nostalgic for some of them, there are many others that we are well rid of.

This is Pollock Road SE17 in 1964. These clotheslines stretching across between buildings used to be a common sight before the advent of the tumble drier

A florist's horse and cart in Cowley Street, Westminster, in 1948

A rag and bone man in 1952, the inspiration for TV's Steptoe and Son

A coalman in 1955

The lamplighter employed by the Gas, Light and Coke Company putting on the lights in the Temple in 1950

A milk cart in Holborn in June 1946

The Clean Air Act in 1956 meant that chimney sweeps became a dying breed in London. This image was taken in 1937

Who will buy this wonderful morning?

I KNOW people still sell things on the streets but there's an awful lot less of it than there used to be.

It's because there were many more markets that there was more of it. That and the fact that, these days, regulations make it harder for people to just set up a business. Hawkers on London streets also added to the atmosphere with their cries.

This photograph of an ice-cream seller was taken in 1950 at around the same time as a bloke came round the streets of Bethnal Green on his bicycle with a large box on the front from which he sold synthetic ice cream. He was called the Oakey Pokey Man and he had this little song he'd sing at the top of his voice. "A halfpenny a half. A penny a large. They're all big pennences and large papers here." Don't ask me what it meant, I've still not worked it out

The internet and mobile phones have probably been the biggest changes in technology in my recent lifetime. During a newspaper strike in April 1955, this news vendor at Kings Cross station sold three-penny sheets containing football pool results and racing programmes

A bagel seller in Whitechapel in 1947

A hot-chestnut hawker in Leicester Square in 1963

I know you still see men standing in Oxford Street with signs pointing to 'cheap bags' or something but they are not proper sandwich board men. This was in Oxford Street in February 1964

Busking characters

There were many more buskers on the street. These days they are mostly down the Underground, rather than outside the stations, as this chap (pictured right) was in 1967 at Sloane Square – neither do many of them play recorders!

Around Tower Hill there used to be many characters that would entertain the crowds at lunchtime. This tattooed man in 1966 certainly drew a big crowd

"THESE BUSKERS IN COVENT GARDEN IN 1948 MAY WELL HAVE BEEN WORLD WAR TWO VETERANS. THERE WERE MANY MORE PEOPLE AROUND WHEN I WAS A KID THAT HAD INJURIES SUSTAINED IN THE WAR"

A nation of shopkeepers

BECAUSE our family business was green grocers, I definitely have a soft spot for old-fashioned shops.

The kind you can go in for a browse and a chat, rather than rushing up and down the aisles of a supermarket. These few pages give a real insight into the way things were… as well as they way they sometimes still are …

Fishmongers would always lay out their wares on a marble slab, with lots of ice to try to keep the fish as fresh as possible. I'm not sure that they ever could on a hot summer's day.
These photographs were taken in 1950

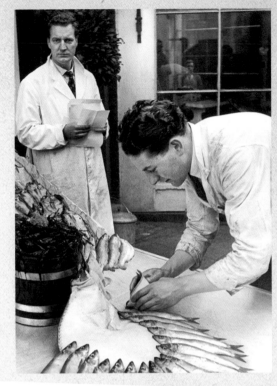

This lady doing her shopping in 1950 naturally had her own bag to take home what she bought. No-one gave you plastic bags and it's good to see the old shopping bag making a bit of a comeback

Door-to-door salesmen were a common thing in post-war Britain, especially as people were rebuilding their lives. This was 1952 and these domestic appliance sellers are interesting people in new fangled gadgets like washing machines and sophisticated gas or electric cookers

This was a common sight in 1955 when this photo was taken. Shopkeepers advertised their wares on their windows in those pre-supermarket days, when women bought groceries on a daily basis

These days, bookmakers are all big chains but the William Massey betting shop, or the much more prosaic 'turf accountant', was in Bethnal Green when I was growing up. This photo dates from 1961

What we did on our holidays

PEOPLE hardly ever went on holiday when I was a kid. We thought ourselves lucky because we had my nan's caravan in Clacton to visit. My mum probably never really went more than 10 miles out of London, other than the visits to Clacton. If you were lucky you took day trips to the seaside.

These people are taking a trip to Margate on a steamer in 1960

A popular day out was a trip to the Derby on Epsom Downs. Huge crowds went every year; many more than attend the Derby today. This is the scene at the Coronation Derby, on June 6, 1953. Jockey Sir Gordon Richards, who was awarded a knighthood in the Queen's Coronation Honours, is congratulated by Queen Elizabeth II after winning the Epsom Derby on racehorse Pinza

Holiday crowds at Waterloo station in July 1960. Another thing that you no longer see, kids of this age wearing shorts!

Because so few people did not have cars the most popular way of going on holiday was by train. Bank holidays, if anything, were even busier as people tried to make the most of the limited days off they had. Have you ever thought why they are called 'holidays'? It's a corruption of holy days, dating from the time when the days on which people did not work, corresponded with Christian celebrations like Easter, Whitsun and Christmas.

What many people from the East End did was to go hop-picking in Kent. While it wasn't a complete holiday it was a big change from life at home and whole families decamped to the countryside for several weeks

Both these photos date from 1930 and give some idea of what the people got up to. When I was looking at these I suddenly thought, you don't see women wearing a headscarf like turbans any longer, it used to be so common in the East End

Londoners making their way to London Bridge station for the first official 'hop pickers' train for the 1945 season

The day we got our telephone

IT seems appropriate to end this chapter with something on telephones as, for me, that's what has changed the way we live now more than anything else.

In 1950, when I was about six, my nan and grandad who we were living with got a telephone; we were one of the first families in our street to get one. They got it, I think, because of their business but it also meant that people would sometimes pop in to use the phone, rather than walk down the road to the nearest phone box to do all that press button A, put your coppers in the box and then press button B when someone answered on the other end. Anyway, the point is we had a phone and like everyone else in London we had a four-digit number.

Like many people my age there are two numbers I always remember. Whitehall 1212 and our own home phone number, which was Advance 3762.

Today, of course, we all have two numbers to remember, our home number and our mobile phone, and of course they are all digits now, there's no name of a telephone exchange to put in front of the numbers, which to my mind made it far easier to remember numbers. Not that I now have to remember numbers, they are all programmed into my phone.

Whitehall 1212 was the number of the Metropolitan Police given out on broadcasts or in the newspaper if there was a crime and the police were seeking information; of course, if it was an emergency you just dialed 999. As a kid, I took for granted that our telephone exchange was Advance – you just dialed the three letters ADV plus the number. I had no idea why it was Advance and it wasn't until many years later I found out why it had the name because, believe me, there was nothing advanced about Bethnal Green.

The actress Jill Ireland using one of the old phone boxes back in 1955; whenever I had to use one I usually stood up

GPO telephonists try out the gas masks as they prepare for any eventuality during A.R.P training

Advance covered the area around Bow and the Mile End Road including Harold Street, where my grandparents lived. Originally, it was to be called Bethnal Green but people objected to the downmarket name and so Advance was picked; it tells you a lot about where I came from.

We were not the only area of London that had a telephone number with an exchange name that had nothing to do with the area that it served. For instance, the area around Westminster had the three-letter prefix ABB, for Abbey, short for Westminster Abbey. Another area near to us, Poplar, was East, short for East End of London. One of my favourite exchanges was Gibbon, which served the Putney area of West London. It's named after Sir Edward Gibbon, the man who wrote The Decline And Fall Of The Roman Empire and was born in Putney.

South of the river was HOP, which was short for nothing but did tell you that in the Southwark area there were a number of Hop merchants and breweries. If you

Mr. Anthony Wedgewood-Benn, before he became plain old Tony Benn, during the time he was the Post Master General, opening a new International Telephone Exchange in London in 1965

want something really unusual try working out why phone numbers in Chislehurst and Bickley, not far from where we moved to in south east London, had an exchange called Imperial, or IMP.

Well, Louis Bonaparte, the only son of Napoleon III by Empress Eugénie, was killed in Zululand while he was attached to the British Expeditionary Force in 1979 and his body was taken back to Chislehurst where it is buried.

Others like LORds, for the area around Maida Vale and Lord's cricket ground are reasonably obvious. Many have perfectly obvious names, like Mayfair or Paddington. Then there's the exotic, LAG, short for Lagoon, which was named after Surbiton Lagoon.

London, like the rest of Britain, had telephone exchanges everywhere, the places where ladies sat at big boards and connected calls.

The old 'press button A and B' phone boxes began to be replaced in 1959 by boxes with phones on which you paid when the person answered the phone. These were necessary following the introduction of STD in major towns, because the old coin-operated boxes could not cope with automatically connected trunk calls.

It was also around this time that phone calls became more automated and the need for telephonists began to reduce, although I still remember when you had to book a call to many overseas countries via the operator. When I first started going abroad on dance trips it was like venturing into the unknown, no-one could get a hold of you and you couldn't just call home.

It was in 1966 that London switched over to all-digit telephone numbers and then in 1990 the old London 01 number was replaced by 07 for inner London and 08 for outer London. Interestingly, Whitehall 1212 is still kind of in use. If you want to contact the Metropolitan Police there number for non-emergency calls is 020 7230 1212.

Grandad always wore a flat cap, they were called cheese cutters; he was never without it, he even slept in it. However, if the telephone rang he took off his hat before saying: "Advance 3762, Albert Eldridge speaking."

In 1969 this lady was Britain's oldest telephonist at 79 years old

This is the police box, one like the Tardis that was close to my grandparents' house in Harold Street, Bethnal Green

"GRANDAD ALWAYS WORE A FLAT CAP.
HE EVEN SLEPT IN IT. HOWEVER, IF THE
TELEPHONE RANG HE TOOK OFF HIS
HAT BEFORE SAYING 'ADVANCE 3762,
ALBERT ELDRIDGE SPEAKING'..."

CHAPTER

8

The business of moving Londoners around the capital as well as bringing in commuters, holidaymakers and visitors has always been a demanding and complex affair. As numbers have increased, so has the technology to make it run smoothly, at least most of the time. Truth is, I marvel at how it all works so very well. Some might complain about the odd delay but then some people just complain for the sake of it . . .

Travelling in style

SINCE first appearing on Dancing With The Stars I've lost count how many times I've flown over the Atlantic between London and Los Angeles – to be honest air travel gets on my wick. If you had said to me in the 1950s and 1960s that I would have been travelling back and forward to America like I have been, I would have thought you were daft. Truth is, no one I knew took trips abroad, and that was true for the vast majority of the population.

In 1966, shortly after buying a new pair of Hush Puppies (for those too young to remember they are a kind of suede shoe and the height of fashion back then) I went abroad. I went with my girlfriend along with her mum and dad, and we went to Spain – separate rooms, thank you!

About the only thing I knew about Spain was it was the place where Real Madrid came from.

We went to a place called Sitges that was a small resort that today is very large and boasts of being 'one of the hippest gay holiday spots in Europe'. Back then we still thought being gay was just being happy.

Our flight was from Gatwick Airport on a Saturday afternoon, which left plenty of time for my girlfriend's mum to go the hairdressers for her regular shampoo and set.

Unlike today when everyone travels casually we were all dressed to the nines; Harry, my girlfriend's dad, was particularly well turned out in an open necked shirt, a paisley cravat, all topped off by a blazer with gold buttons.

Regardless of never having been on a plane before, I don't remember much about the flight itself, but I do remember the aircraft had propellers.

My point is to let you know just how different it all was. What we now take for granted, really was an adventure.

While it may not be an adventure travelling by bus, tube or train it's now a much cleaner experience and less taxing in many ways. London's stations may have sounded all glamorous with their steam trains and 'Brief Encounter' moments but give me modern day St Pancras any day.

Mind you I wouldn't have minded taking the Golden Arrow to Paris. Then again, the Channel Tunnel is a lot better than a ferry crossing to France in the middle of winter.

These horse-drawn buses in Piccadilly in 1904 were nearing the end of their working life

On the buses... and trams

TODAY there are over 6 million bus journeys taken every working day in London, from one of 19,500 bus stops in the capital, meaning 90 per cent of Londoners live within 250 yards of one of them.

Over the years they have been all kinds of different trams and buses to transport us around the capital. Not sure about being on the open-topped buses in the wind and rain.

Horse-drawn carriages and buses in The Strand in 1908

Oxford Street in 1926

An Omnibus in September 1909 heading for Oxford Street

Trams running along the embankment below the Shell Mex building, in December 1932. Shell Mex house had only opened the year before, on the site of the Hotel Cecil and stands behind the original facade of the Hotel and between the Adelphi and the Savoy Hotel

"THE FAMOUS TICKET MACHINES HAD A LONG ROLL OF PAPER INSIDE THAT ALWAYS SEEMED TO NEED CHANGING WHEN IT CAME TIME FOR ME TO PAY MY FARE"

Trams and buses ran on different routes but this one was going nowhere in March 1933 after it suffered a puncture

A London bus can still make it through, despite the road looking more like a canal

A bus conductor in 1960 with one of the famous ticket machines that had a long roll of paper inside that always seemed to need changing when it came time for me to pay my fare

London's trams finished running in July 1952 and this was an event marking their demise

Charing Cross Underground station in November 1950. One of the best developments on the Tube is that stations and trains are now much brighter and less claustrophobic than they used to be

An Underground carriage in 1946

Going underground

OVER 1.1 billion people use the tube in a year, that's over 3 million every day going through over 270 stations displayed on the legendary Underground map that was designed by Harry Beck in 1931.

There's nothing lost about the Underground, it is as vital today as it has been for over a century. London can boast the first underground railway in the world, dating from 1863 it is now part of the Circle, Hammersmith & City and Metropolitan lines; it was also the first to have electric trains, in 1890.

Apparently Mrs June Clark of Avenscroft Road, Chiswick, W4, used to take her own stool to travel to and from work on the underground in July 1953. According to Mrs Clark: "Men just won't give up their seats to women nowadays, so I decided a few weeks ago to carry my own". Do men give up their seats on the Underground today?

The memorial for the men, women and children that died in Bethnal Green Underground Station

Bethnal Green tragedy that touched our family

WHEN I was very young, my dad told me about a tragedy that hit Bethnal Green during the war, something that touched every family living in the area.

Work on building Bethnal Green tube station had started in 1936 when the Central line was extended from Liverpool Street. When war broke out it was still unfinished. Throughout the Blitz it was used as an air raid shelter; inside were 5,000 bunks and it could accommodate 7,000 people.

In early 1943, the bombing of London was not as intense, but after the RAF bombed Berlin on March 1, there was an expectation that the Nazis would retaliate; when the sirens sounded two days later, there was little surprise.

By November 1943 people had got very used to sheltering in the tubes, although raids did tail off between the first Blitz and later in the war when German V-2 and V-1 rockets were raining down on London

Three buses stopped to allow their passengers to seek shelter in the underground station shelter. As the passengers were hurrying down the steps, a woman holding a baby fell down the stairs that led to the platforms, and a man tripped over her just as there was a shout from the top of the stairs that bombs were falling. Simultaneously there was a deafening noise, not actually a bomb at all, but a new kind of anti-aircraft gun that was fired from close by. It all led to panic. There was pushing and shoving and with 300 or more people stuck in the stairwell the inevitable happened, people started to fall as more frightened people crammed into the confined space.

When it was all over, 101 adults and 62 children were dead from suffocation; 60 more people were taken to hospital. My mum's cousin, the boxer, Dickie Corbett was one of the dead; he was at home in Bethnal Green on leave from the army.

Years later I found out from a lady that helped to raise money for a permanent memorial that Dickie's real name was Richard Coleman, and that's the name that is on the memorial.

Nurses giving people sheltering in the Underground an anti-flu medicine in January 1941

Come fly with me

FRANK Sinatra is one of my favourite singers and his invitation to "come fly with me" is still one of the best songs about going travelling, although I have to say that flying backwards and forwards to Hollywood for Dancing With The Stars is not as glamorous as you think it might be.

When Sinatra released that album in 1958 most people could only dream of air travel; foreign travel was for the rich and famous, of course, Sinatra qualified on both counts.

By the end of 1958, more than a million passengers made the trip across the Atlantic by air – the first year that aircraft carried more passengers across the Atlantic than the liners – something that had been considered a preposterous thought only a decade earlier.

This was Croydon Airport in July 1929 when the French aviator Louis Bleriot arrived to celebrate 30 years since he first flew across the English Channel

The De Havilland Comet was the world's first commercial jet airliner to reach production and is seen here in BOAC livery leaving London Heathrow for Johannesburg on the world's first scheduled jet air service on May 2, 1952. BOAC was one of the two companies that eventually created British Airways. In 1952, Heathrow airport handled under a million passengers in a full year

London's original airport was at Croydon, which was then in Surrey. It opened in 1923 and expanded during the pre-war era to handle flights to many European cities, at least the ones in range of the aircraft.

With the outbreak of war, it became a fighter base during the Battle of Britain and in the post war period its position as London's airport was usurped by, first, Northolt and then Heathrow.

In 1950 the government decided that Gatwick should become an additional London airport, but it was not until the 1960s that it really began to become anything approaching a major airport, passing 2 million passengers for the first time in 1968.

Today Gatwick handles over 34 million passengers, annually. Meanwhile Heathrow has continued to expand to the point where it handles over 70 million passengers every year.

Way before Richard Branson's Virgin Atlantic Airways appeared on the scene, Freddie Laker did so much to pioneer cheap travel to America. Laker is seen here at Gatwick Airport on September 26, 1977 when his Skytrain service was inaugurated to New York

"WHEN FRANK SINATRA RELEASED 'COME FLY WITH ME' IN 1958, MOST PEOPLE COULD ONLY DREAM OF AIR TRAVEL. FOREIGN TRAVEL WAS FOR THE RICH AND FAMOUS"

Short S.45 Solent 2 was the last of the large flying boat to be flown by BOAC on overseas routes. It first flew in 1946 and the last one was built in 1949. This photograph was taken on May 5, 1949 when the Lord Mayor, Sir George Aylwen, named the aircraft City of London in celebration of 30 years of British civil air transport

"COMMERCIAL SEAPLANES NEVER
DID OPERATE FROM THE THAMES,
DESPITE SEVERAL SCHEMES
BEING PUT FORWARD TO MAKE IT
A REALITY. IN 1987, LONDON CITY
AIRPORT OPENED AND NOW HANDLES
OVER 3 MILLION PASSENGERS ON
OVER 250 FLIGHTS EVERY DAY"

In the late 1930s, the competition to fly the North Atlantic, mainly to deliver the mail quickly, was intense. Short Brothers came up with this novel idea of an aircraft that piggybacked another to allow it to have sufficient range to make the crossing. The Mayo composite aircraft, as it was called, is seen here during taxi-ing trials along the River Medway on January 19, 1938. On February 6, 1938, it flew for the first time and after further successful tests, the first transatlantic flight was made on 21 July 1938. War got in the way of any serious development time for the idea. Who said the Americans had all the best ideas?

The magic of steam

RAILWAY stations always held a fascination for me as a young kid, probably because we didn't really go anywhere on a train.

The great London stations were the most glamorous terminal, taking people to the Continent from Waterloo and bringing people to London who landed at Plymouth or Southampton on the great ocean-going liners that carried people to the four corners of the world in the days when commercial air travel was still in its infancy.

With steam trains operating all the long distance routes, as well as some of the short routes, it meant that stations were dark smoke and soot filled places with atmosphere you could touch, and of course smell.

On the positive side the smoke filled stations made for great photo opportunities.

The Flying Scotsman leaving Kings Cross station on its first non-stop run to Scotland in May 1928

This London & North Western Railway Claughton class 4-6-0 locomotive, leaving Euston station in April 1928

Queen Mary opening Waterloo station in March 1922

Liverpool Street station in the 1950s

Most journeys to Europe from London started at Victoria station. Seen here is Winston Churchill with Lord Wodehouse on his way to Paris in January 1925

The Golden Arrow train service that went from Victoria station to Dover and then, after a ferry crossing to Calais, passengers were taken on the French equivalent to Paris. After ceasing to operate during World War Two the service was restarted in 1946, when this photo was taken; the all-Pullman train departed from Victoria at 10.30, reaching the Gare du Nord in Paris at 17.30, and from Paris at 12.15, arriving in Victoria at 19.30

This photograph from May 1921 shows members of the Old Cab Drivers Association driving cabs around Lincoln Inns Fields to demonstrate they were still capable of handling a horse drawn Hackney carriage

Taxi for Goodman!

TECHNICALLY speaking, a London taxi is a Hackney carriage. The first Hackney carriage licenses were issued in 1662 for horse drawn carriages that were, by 1834, called Hansom cabs. These, just like today, were vehicles for hire.

Electric Hackney carriages made a brief late-19th century appearance before motorised cabs were introduced in 1901. However, it was a slow and gradual change over from horse power to the combustion engine as the last horse-drawn cabs were phased out in 1947. The motorised cab has gone through many different designs to the point where some London cabs are almost unrecognisable as cabs, apart from their distinctive orange 'for hire' sign.

Taxi drivers protesting in Whitehall in September 1978 over a 28% fare rise they had been awaiting for 15 months

A cab outside the Dorchester Hotel, in Park Lane, in July 1961. It's the kind with the open area for the carriage of luggage that was a feature of all motorised cabs up until the 1970s

A state-of-the-art taxi in June 1933

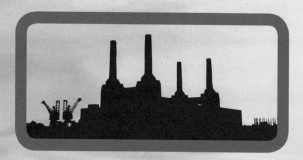

BUILDING
SIGHTS

This lovely sunset scene, featuring Tower Bridge, was taken in 1966 when London really did look a very different city. So many new buildings have sprung up in the past 50 years, some from necessity, some for reasons I don't understand, but it has made views across the London skyline unimaginably different to someone like my old Grandad – sometimes it seems like it's changing year by year. While conservation has saved many buildings, many have been lost, not always a bad thing but there's always a price to pay for progress . . .

The outside of the old factory, now Bow Quarter. The blue plaque outside the entrance commemorates Annie Besant who led the industrial action at the match factory

Staten Building

Park Buildings

Arlington Building

Lexington Building

Manhattan Building

The Match Girls Strike of 1888
was led here by

ANNIE BESANT

Journalist and Lecturer

1847 - 1933

Following the strike, Annie Besant became
Secretary of the new Matchmakers Union.
In 1917 she became President of the Indian
National Congress and was also International
President of the Theosophical Society
from 1907 - 1933

I LOVE walking around London, there are always interesting buildings to see and if you look up, rather than watching the pavement, you will see the blue plaques that tell you who may have lived in a particular building, as well as other features that give you an insight into the history of the capital's amazing architecture.

There are all kinds of small streets, alleyways and the like tucked away that are there to be explored. Cutting down these small side streets and alleys will often lead you to places that tell you so much of our rich and varied history.

Let me tell you about one example of rebuilding that has turned out well. The old Bryant & May match factory in the East End flourished, if that's the right word, from mid-19th century well into the middle part of the 20th. In 1888 the girls that worked in the factory went on strike against their 14-hour days, money and conditions but most of all because of the awful health issues brought on by working with white phosphorus. The buildings were reconstructed in 1910 when more than 2,000 girls worked there; it closed in 1979, when numbers had dwindled to less than 300.

The site fell into disrepair until it was rebuilt in the late 1980s and renamed Bow Quarter as one of the first urban regeneration projects in the East End. Today, Bow Quarter has more than 700 apartments and some former workers' cottages, all set in seven acres.

It's a real triumph of regenerating old into new and, best of all, it remembers the sacrifices made by those women and while their London may be lost, I think that's no bad thing.

BBC Broadcasting
House in May 1953

Here is the news... BBC is bombed

WHENEVER I walk through the doors of Broadcasting House I feel like I'm stepping back in time. In my head I hear a voice saying, "This is the BBC. Here is the news." Walking up to the front of this beautiful art deco building it kind of puts me in the mood for whatever I'm there to do.

The Corporation's London HQ in Portland Place was opened in May 1932 and with its facade of Portland stone, it shined brilliant white. During World War Two it was painted in a drab camouflage to make it less of a target to the Luftwaffe, despite this it still received several hits, including one in October 1940.

The 500-pound delayed action bomb entered through a window of a room on the seventh floor that housed the switchboard at around 8.15pm, crashed through walls and floors before coming to rest in the music library on the fifth floor, where it was found at around 8.30pm. Half-an-hour later, just after Bruce Belfrage began reading the 9 o'clock news in the basement studio, someone tried moving the bomb. He had got as far as saying, "the postscript tonight…" when there was a smothered sound of an explosion and Belfrage paused. Lord Lloyd of Dolobran, in the studio to give the postscript, was heard saying, somewhat urgently: "It's all right." Belfrage carried on with the news, and as one paper later reported, was "quickly gathering confidence". There were seven BBC employees, including three women, killed by the blast.

The Shot Tower, used in the making of lead shot for shooting, was originally part of the Lambeth Lead Works that stood between Waterloo Bridge and Hungerford Bridge, on the site of what is now the Queen Elizabeth Hall. It was built in 1826 and remained in operation until 1949. It was the only existing building to be retained on the site of the Festival of Britain. I remember seeing it when I went to the festival in 1951. The tower was demolished to make way for the Queen Elizabeth Hall in 1967. Our photo shows the tower in October 1959, next to the Royal Festival Hall

"FINALLY, IT SEEMS THE SITE IS TO BE REDEVELOPED, AND IT IS TO RETAIN THE FOUR TOWERS THAT ARE SO MUCH A PART OF THE LONDON SKYLINE"

Towers with staying power

IS there a more iconic industrial building in any city in Britain? The old Battersea Power Station, seen here, floodlit for the Festival of Britain in May 1951, was opened in 1933.

Sir Giles Gilbert Scott, a noted architect who had also designed the red telephone box and Liverpool Anglican Cathedral, designed the exterior. He also designed another London power station, Bankside, which now houses the Tate Modern art gallery.

Battersea Power station closed in March 1975 and has been the cause of numerous speculative schemes to see it revitalised. Finally, it seems the site is to be redeveloped, and it is to retain the four towers that are so much a part of the London skyline.

Gone but not forgotten

The original main gate for Old Scotland Yard, just off Whitehall, seen here in 1949. It was originally the headquarters of the Metropolitan Police and its name goes back to it being the lodging place of Scottish kings when they visited London – during those periods when England and Scotland were not at war. The Met left here in 1890 but took the name with them to various other locations before settling on New Scotland Yard just off Victoria Street.

Seen here in 1959, this arch formed the entrance to Euston train station until it was demolished in 1961 as part of wider refurbishment of the area. Its destruction was not without controversy and even today there are campaigning groups that want to see this iconic arch rebuilt

The Royal Aquarium and Winter Garden opened in 1876 was located to the west of Westminster Abbey. Inside there was a theatre and around the main hall were rooms for eating, reading and even for playing chess, as well as an art gallery and a skating rink. Sadly, despite an elaborate water supply system the aquarium never did have any fish in it, although it is said that a dead whale was once put on display there. The building was demolished in 1903 and now Westminster Hall stands on the site

Prefabricated houses were a necessity after the end of World War Two, especially in the East End. These prefabs, photographed in 1946, are on the Isle of Dogs – an area that now forms part of Docklands. The houses were seen as temporary but stayed up for much longer than originally anticipated

How the Fleet Street story began

FLEET Street derives its name from the River Fleet that rises in Hampstead and enters the Thames near New Bridge Street; contrary to popular belief it does not run along the route of one of London's most famous streets. Publishing began in Fleet Street around 1500 when one of Caxton's apprentices set up a printing shop near Shoe Lane.

More printers and publishers followed to serve the many legal firms located at the Inns of Court. By 1702, the Daily Courant, London's first daily newspaper, was published in Fleet Street. By the 20th century most of Britain's national daily papers were located on or adjacent to Fleet Street but by 1988 they had all moved out. Nevertheless, we all still refer to Fleet Street as the home of newspapers, you wonder how long it will last?

The Daily Mirror's building decorated to celebrate VJ Day to mark the end of World War Two. The Daily Mirror, like most newspapers, moved to Docklands and is now based at Canary Wharf

The Cock Tavern in Fleet Street, a pub frequented by both Samuel Pepys and Charles Dickens, as well as some newspapermen, seen here during the 1930s

Delivery vans of the London Evening
News wait for the paper to roll off the
presses in Fleet Street in 1961

The Daily
Telegraph's offices
were completed in
1930 and are seen
here in 1955

Westminster Abbey on May 12, 1937 at the Coronation of King George VI

Robbing Peter to pay Paul

DID you know that Westminster Abbey is not its proper name? It is, correctly, the Collegiate Church of St Peter at Westminster and it is the origin of the phrase "to rob Peter to pay Paul".

Following Henry VIII's death, his son Edward VI continued with his father's work of redistributing the money and the assets of the old monasteries. St Peter's was apparently left destitute by an over-spending bishop and was always asking the king for more money which eventually irritated him so much that he took away revenue that it had been deriving from the Manor of Paddington and gave it to St Paul's.

St Paul's Cathedral in 1947. From 1710, when it was built by Sir Christopher Wren, until 1962, it was the tallest building in London

Bridging the gap

THE history of London's bridges is a complex one and demands a book all of its own. Down the centuries, crossing the Thames has been achieved in a variety of ways, starting with boatman who rowed you across, which even continued after the early bridges were built.

Once bridge-building became a reality across the width of the Thames, bridges were built regularly with the heyday of what we see today occurring in the late 18th and 19th century, with a few notable exceptions. Of course, there's also been ferries and tunnels and even new major crossings like the Dartford Crossing, a bridge dear to my heart as it allows me to get to and from the north, directly from my dance studio!

London Bridge itself, or at least something called London Bridge, has existed in roughly the same place for around 2,000 years. The first stone bridge was constructed in 1209 – this is the famous one that is depicted in old paintings showing buildings perched atop of it. After 600 years it was finally decided a new one was needed and in 1831 the latest incarnation was opened and the old medieval bridge was demolished. Sadly, the 1831 bridge began to sink, clearly not such good engineers as their medieval counterparts, and it was sold to an American, who had it taken down piece by piece so that it could be reconstructed in Arizona, in the United States, where, today, it is a tourist attraction. Queen Elizabeth II opened the bridge we all see now in 1973.

Old London Bridge in 1965

This, the original Waterloo Bridge, was opened in 1817 but from 1884 serious problems were found after the river flow had increased following the closure of the London Bridge with the houses on top. It all led to work going on for 50 years to maintain the bridge. Eventually, a decision was taken to build a new one and the architect, Sir Giles Gilbert Scott, who also designed Battersea Power Station, was brought in to design it. This partially opened in 1942 and was finished after the war ended; it was the only London bridge to be damaged by German bombing. The picture shows the heavily supported arches in 1934, shortly before the old bridge was demolished

This view of the Thames in August 1959 shows Waterloo Bridge in the foreground, Blackfriars Railway Bridge, Southwark Bridge, Cannon Street Rail Bridge, London Bridge and finally Tower Bridge

CHAPTER

10

Before the 1960s, the West End really was the glamorous part of London. Not that it isn't today, it was just more so back then. The gulf between the heady West End and the East End, as well as the areas around London was enormous. It really was a case of 'bright lights, big city' . . .

COMING from the East End, that's what we used to say if someone went to the smart bit of London – the West End. When I say, if someone went, I really mean someone else. Certainly, no-one in my family ever thought of going to the West Ends for a night out. I'm not sure my grandad and grandma ever went there, despite it only being a few miles away.

Soho is principally the parallel roads, Wardour Street, Dean Street, Frith Street and Greek Street. Bordered as it is by Oxford Street to the north and Regent Street to the west, Charing Cross Road to the east and Shaftesbury Avenue to the south, it has the feel of an enclave. Its village feel is emphasised by the fact that it even has its own village square.

The name is said to come from a hunting cry and that the 1st Duke of Monmouth used it as a rallying call for his men at the Battle of Sedgemoor in 1685 but this area of London was already known as Soho.

French Huguenots came to this part of London in the late 17th century, built a church in Soho Square and in World War Two the Free French forces, based in London, used the York Minster pub in Dean Street – General De Gaulle is said to have written his famous rallying speech for the French in the pub. It's now known as the French House. Both Brendan Behan and Dylan Thomas wrote and drank in the pub.

Soho's fall from respectable grace began in the mid-19th century and, by the early 20th century, many foreign-owned restaurants had opened in the area.

It became something of a by-word for decadence and the whole seedy side of Soho, with its sex clubs, added to its allure for some. Whatever happened, it never lost its appeal and with the many music clubs that opened it attracted people for both entertainment and for eating.

Like Soho, Shepherd Market lies tucked away, a little further to the west, in fashionable Mayfair. In the 18th century an architect named Edward Shepherd was commissioned to develop the area, that had previously been a market, and from then until the 1920s it was a fashionable part of London. On the edge of Shepherd Market was Half Moon Street where the writer P.G. Wodehouse had the home of his fictional character, Bertie Wooster. It later gained a reputation as something a little more racy when it became an area frequented by, albeit high-class, prostitutes.

Today, Shepherd's Market is once again an upmarket area but has still not quite lost its village atmosphere.

The corner of Frith Street and Old Compton Street, London

Carnival fun

SOHO was so like a village that it even had its own carnival. It's also an area of London that has attracted eccentrics, artists, writers and musicians so it is no wonder that the area has survived as its own little micro-community.

Even today, as you walk into the area it's like crossing some invisible line and once you are on the other side things can happen. In the mid-1950s the Soho Carnival or Fair became something of an annual event with floats as well as some unusual races.

The waiter's race in 1955

Like every carnival it had its own Carnival Queen, this is from 1960

Soho Carnival in full swing, July 1955

Dancing in the street in July 1956

*Old Compton Street,
Soho, in the mid-1950s*

Dean Street, Soho, in the mid-1950s

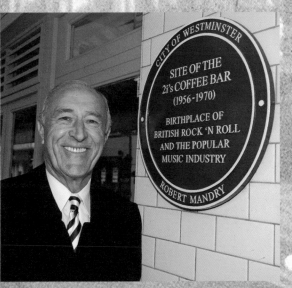

"SOHO BECAME SOMETHING OF A BY-WORD FOR DECADENCE AND THE WHOLE SEEDY SIDE ADDED TO ITS ALLURE FOR SOME. WHATEVER HAPPENED, IT NEVER LOST ITS APPEAL AND WITH THE MUSIC CLUBS THAT OPENED, IT ATTRACTED PEOPLE FOR BOTH ENTERTAINMENT AND FOR EATING"

Shepherd Market in July 1948

City of Westminster.
SHEPHERD MARKET. *W.*
LEADING TO WHITEHORSE STREET & PICCADILLY.

The arch leading from Curzon Street into the market in 1955

A woman dining at a restaurant at Shepherd Market in July 1948

It's awfully quiet here

BACK in 1925 Shepherd Market was described as "one of the oddest incongruities in London".

The fact is it remains the same today, so in a sense this area of London is not lost, it's just different. What's lost about it is the fact that few people who are not looking for it, find it. The streets surrounding it, somehow, conspire to prevent you from locating it and when you do it seems awfully quiet for London.

Just around the corner from Shepherd Market is the house in which both Cass Elliot of The Mamas and Papas died in 1974, and then four years later, Keith Moon, the drummer with The Who, also died in the same property.

Window-shopping at Shepherd Market

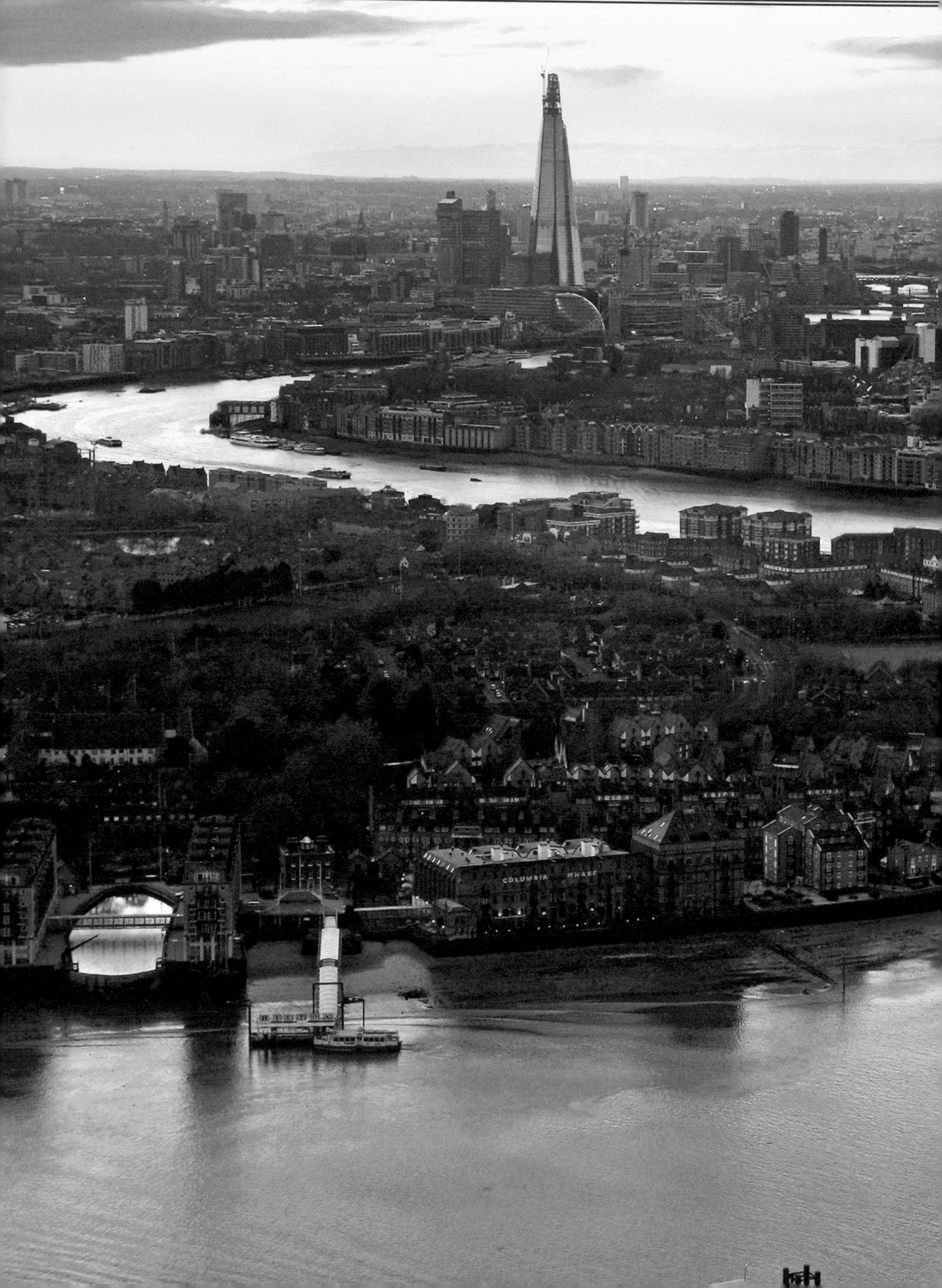
COLUMBIA WHARF

As a kid I went to play in Greenwich Park many times and the view in the 1950s and even 1960s was just like you see in the photo from 1934. Just look at how it has changed; what's occurred is way beyond anything my nan and grandad could have ever imagined. It's progress but what all of us must try to hang onto is what was good about the past, while embracing what's good about today and what's to come in the future

No place like home

Now, I'm sure that those of you that have watched me on the television will know I like a good old saying. And there's one saying that I would love to have been the one to have thought up – "When a man is tired of London, he is tired of life; for there is in London all that life can afford." It was Samuel Johnson who came up with this, way back in 1777, and it remains as true today as it obviously was nearly 250 years ago.

I hope that this book will have given you some insight into just why I love London and have enjoyed calling it home for the past sixty-something years. When I was young, I loved London, and particularly the East End, because it was my playground, the place where I began to learn about life and just what an exciting place it was to live. As I grew into a teenager, and started work, I found endless opportunities to enjoy myself in London; whether through sport, entertainment or just socialising with my mates.

When I began dancing, London provided so many places for me to compete as well as the fun that Ballroom and Latin dancing gave me. As I became a little more successful and my lifestyle changed, and began travelling around the world, I found that London was still the most attractive city on earth.

Growing older I became more and more interested in history and that's when I found just how much London has to offer. Around every corner there are buildings, blue plaques, hidden alleyways and things to learn about – the possibilities to be fascinated by London are endless.

So let me finish by giving you another old saying, this one from a song that was inspired by the doodlebugs that stopped me from actually being born within the sound of Bow Bells. It was composed by Hubert Gregg and made into a hit by Flanagan and Allen.

"Maybe it's because I'm a Londoner, that I love London so." Maybe I wasn't born in London but no-one will ever convince me that I'm anything but a Londoner.

"London goes beyond any boundary or convention. It contains every wish or word ever spoken, every action or gesture ever made, every harsh or noble statement ever expressed. It is illimitable. It is Infinite London."

– Peter Ackroyd, London: The Biography